"Those Were the Days"

Thanks for sharing this with me.

"Dad"

Mark A. Jacobs

D1711932

"Those Were the Days"

Aviation Adventures of
World War II

Mark A. Savage

Avatar Publishing
7516 Slate Ridge Boulevard
Reynoldsburg, Ohio 43068

Copyright © **Avatar Publishing**

Library of Congress Cataloging in Publication Data.

ISBN: 0-89894-041-9

Photo Acknowledgement Robert Foose

Cover Design by Robert Tourt   Columbus, Ohio
Typesetting by Composition Services   New York, New York

10 9 8 7 6 5 4 3 2 1

Printed in The United States of America

Mark A. Savage

Dedicated to

THOSE   . . . . kids who loved their country and especially loved to fly.

WERE   . . . . it not for their many personal sacrifices, we wouldn't have it so good.

THE   . . . . field of aviation has been enriched by their enthusiasm and knowledge.

DAYS   . . . . of sacrifice and frustrations were readily given in order that we may all enjoy freedom.

Introduction

I have been privileged to call General Paul W. Tibbets a real true friend. We have known each other for many years. When I approached Paul with regards to writing a personal introduction to this book, he said to me, "You know, I have a special place in my heart for you fighter pilots and I will let you know after I finish reading it."

I am sure most of you will recall Paul Tibbets as the Command Pilot of the B-29, The Enola Gay. He and his crew were the first to drop the Atom Bomb on Hiroshima, Japan.

After reading my book, he presented me with the following letter expressing his personal feelings.

I hope you too will equally share in the adventures and excitement of that era. Beyond a shadow of a doubt, the events of **Those Were The Days,** will never happen again.

Foreword

The Enola Gay
(Photo courtesy U.S. Air Force Museum.)

Mark A. (Doc) Savage concludes his book with SENTIMENTAL JOURNEY. However, as I started reading I found myself embarking on one. Anyone familiar with the "routine" of becoming a Flying Cadet (Pre-WWII) will be able to relate and probably relive some of Doc's experiences. As I read the book it brought back many recollections of things almost forgotten after all these years.

Of particular note is the affection shown by Savage for some of those old airplanes. In their day they were "the best" and each had its own distinc-

tive characteristics, both flying and sound. *Many of us are lucky that we became familiar with and had our unique experiences with them because they are a vanished breed. Those not familiar with those "old birds" will never know the thrill of the sound of screaming wires and struts; the wind-up and high pitch of a propeller reving up to the tune of those jugs belching out flame and exhaust. They will never experience the joy of "feeling" an airplane fly. Those of us like Doc, will carry that knowledge on our last solo.*

Following Savage through training and into the early phases of WWII, you can't but help to wonder how he, or any of us, ever made it. We all have had the number one co-pilot with us because, based on the things we experienced and lived, tell, or write about, the reader will be left with the belief that it was a case of the "blind leading the blind".

Savage had a varied flying career during the period 1941–45. He started out in dive bombers and then to the ferry command where he gained more valuable experience in flying through a number of different type airplanes and a constant mix of conditions under which they were flown. Maybe not as "glamourous" as combat, but a better opportunity to become a better airman. The reader has but to "ride" with him through some of these experiences to see how he gained in becoming an experienced airman, capable of more positive control through better planning.

Finally as one goes through the pages from beginning to end, you will sense the development and maturity of Mark Savage as was the case for so many thousands of young men at that time. He correctly conveys the experience of accelerated maturity brought on by the camaraderie and emotions of living from day to day; seeing your buddies die all around you and wondering when your number is to be called. Correctly, in my opinion, he shows the attitude prevalent at that time of "fighting hard, then playing hard" because "tomorrow you may die". Such a scenario is the only way one could keep his sanity to face the tomorrow. Mark Savage has taken us from "the beginning to end" of a rare emotional experience with airplanes and airmen.

Paul W. Tibbets
Brig. Gen. U.S. Air Force Ret.

Preface

A re these stories fact or fiction? Without a doubt they are all true. This has been written for you the reader to enjoy some of the many adventures of a pilot who spent four years in the U.S. Air Force; three years overseas, with one year in combat in the 12th Air Force in W.W. II. Despite all the frustrations and fears, there were the good times too.

The Air Force provided a platform for me to make a career and life in the field of aviation. Upon my discharge, I went on to college at Kent State University, Kent, Ohio. Then after four plus years, I returned to my first love full time, the field of aviation.

With over 17,000 hours, I'm still actively engaged flying in the business world of aviation, having flown all types of aircraft, including the Lear Jet.

I am currently the Governor of the Soaring Society of America for the State of Ohio. I've built and still fly my own high performance sailplane.

I owe so much to my wife, Ruth, who is quite understanding and willing to wait for her wayward pilot-husband to come home at all hours of the day or night.

Many of my friends have been after me for years to write about my aviation adventures. With 24 chapters completed in this book, there are still many more to be written.

I would like to acknowledge my old friend and colleague the Reverend Doctor Roland W. Tapp, who has encouraged and helped guide me in the completion of this book. I owe him a special word of thanks, as this book would not have been possible without his help.

A number of photos came from my own collection, but I would be remiss if I failed to give Bob Cooper credit for helping me assemble and photograph the many pictures seen within.

A personal thanks to the United States Air Force Museum for giving me permission to use some of their pictures that appear in this book.

One last important point. The names of some of the characters have been changed, for reasons known only to this author.

Table of Contents

*"It's today's dreams
that make our tomorrows."*

Chapter 1
The Early Days

A viation has always had a strong hold on me. I can hardly remember when I never thought or wanted to do anything but fly. This particular feeling exists even today.

Going back in time, the very first recollection of my first flight occurred when I was just four years old. We lived in an old two-story house and this particular day was one that burned itself in my memory forever. It was about mid-morning and my brother and I were up-stairs jumping on the bed, each trying to see how high we could go. As I jumped on the bed I felt myself going forward and out over the edge. The next thing I knew I crashed through the window screen and out the window. Flashing past the lower kitchen window, I can still see and hear my Mother wide-eyed and screaming, at the sink. The next scene, I'm looking up at all the giants looking down at me.

Gathering me up, they rushed me off to the local hospital. A thorough exam failed to find a single broken bone or bruise. "Incredible, Mr. and Mrs. Savage, your son has just experienced a real miracle!" exclaimed the examining physician.

Later on, my Mother told me that I was always troubled with constipation. After that adventure I had no more trouble and was perfectly normal.

Growing up on the East Coast, I was exposed to aviation in its infant days.

When the word came that the famous dirigible Von Hindenburg was due to fly over, we all stood outdoors and gasped at the tremendous vehicle. Just imagine! It was arriving non-stop all the way from Germany. It actually cast a large shadow on the ground equivalent to the size of a football field as it passed overhead. The engines bleating out their uneven sounds could be heard for miles and miles away.

During the summer, we were always on the alert for the week-end air shows. The old bi-planes would fly overhead releasing thousands of air show leaflets advising of the date, place and time of the: *"Next Big Show!"*

"Find the lucky ticket and get a FREE PASS!" were the words printed on each sheet. Those two words alone created an almost frenzied effort on our part to collect as many leaflets as we could, hoping to find that free pass. Sure it was a come-on, but it worked that way for everyone. The main idea was to get the people thinking *Air-Show.*

That particular summer in '38 went very fast and winter arrived early. About the only thing that ever got me to take notice now was the regular runs over my house by Eastern Airlines with its Curtiss Condor. It was a large bi-wing twin-engine 18 passenger plane.

That winter produced excellent conditions for ice skating. We (our gang) found Mead's Pond at its finest. Our parents were worried as this pond happened to be one of the deepest fresh water ponds in the area. No need to worry today, it's very cold and the ice is clear.

Skating and playing hockey there most of the day, we failed to notice that the ice was weakened and approaching the dangerous level due to all of the skaters now on the pond.

It was late afternoon when it happened. The ice let go in the middle of the pond. There in the center and in the open hole was Stanley Wanlass, a tall 6 foot boy now standing on the very tips of his racer skates, water up to the edge of his chin, yelling, *"Please, some one help me!"* I can't believe my eyes. A large group surround the area afraid to go any closer yet no one is trying to do a thing to help get him out. This time he begs pathetically, *"Please! . . . Please! . . . won't someone help me!"*

I found a large hocky stick and half ran and skated over to the area. Lying on my stomach, I stuck the big hockey stick out to Stan and yelled, *"Grab on!"*

My brother holding on to my skates kept me from sliding into the same open hole. The ice beneath me begins to crack and give. I feel the water creeping up and starting to cover the lower part of my body that is next to

A left echelon of P-26's better known as the "Pea Shooter" as described in "*The Early Days*". (Photo courtesy Bill Sweet collection.)

the ice. It looks like I'm about to join Stan in the frigid water. Stan is hanging on for dear life and saying, "*Thanks, thanks,*" but we are not out yet, as the ice starts to very slowly settle down.

I feel myself and Stan, who now is desperately hanging on to the end of the hockey stick, gradually being dragged back from the sagging ice and open water.

Finally, a loud roar from the crowd greets us as soon as we are clear and on firm ice. Everyone crowds around Stan covering him with blankets and giving him warm drinks while rushing him off to a warm waiting car. I stare in utter disbelief. In the excitement both my brother and I are overlooked in our wet clothes and numbed condition.

We take off our skates in silence and start the long two mile walk home alone.

About all we can tell our folks was, "Sorry we got home so late and no, we did not fall in the pond." No need for explanations now as we are both thankful we got off the pond without losing our lives.

Then in early Spring of '39, my Uncle Weeks, a Major in the Army Air Corps, started flying over our area almost every weekend. His three-ship "V" element formation got just about everyone out of the house. It did a lot to get me motivated and excited about joining the Army Air Corps. These P-26 "Peashooters" made a beautiful sight as they flew over the area. We were not aware of it, but WW II was rapidly approaching the U.S. The Army Air Corps represented the finest for the country with the P-26-E's. A Squadron was based on Long Island, N.Y. and made regular flights over the area. The Squadron with its beautiful "V" ship formations would always arouse attention from everyone. Swinging over to the echelon formation presented a spectacular sight. The Armonk Airport located in White Plains, N.Y., was known as "the small airport in the woods."

There was a lot of flying in those days with many frequent visits from the P-26's, along with the Ford Tri-Motor, parachute jumpers and passenger rides. Everyone looked forward to the week-end air shows.

My uncle was on active duty with the Army Air Corps and every time he flew over was a particular thrill for me. He was my idol. I had a dream that someday I would be a pilot flying fighters. His flying helped fire my ambition more than ever. Finally I contacted my aunt whose cousin was Major Weeks. She knew of my dreams and called him to set up an appointment for me. I felt that if I could talk to him personally, he would be able to guide me towards my goal, *A pair of Silver Wings.*

I eagerly looked forward to that day, and now I'm standing on his front porch waiting to personally meet him. I can hardly contain my excitement. It seemed like an eternity before he answered my ringing at the door. A medium size man greeted me. Dark hair, blue eyes and all dressed up in his Army Air Corps uniform.

He had on his big shiny leather flying boots, pink riding pants, khaki shirt with gold oak leaves on each shoulder. No tie. Wow! I can hardly believe that he is willing to give me his time and advice about getting into the Army Air Corps. We shook hands and walked into his parlor. I formally began by introducing myself to him as one of his related kin. Then I said, "Uncle Roy, I would like to be a pilot in the Air Corps." Nothing like getting right to the point.

That's when the shit hit the fan and I was really put in my place with, "Son . . . I'm Major Weeks." That little remark went over like a lead balloon. From here on the conversation went down hill.

I was still in high school, and he said, "Son, for one thing you can't get into the cadets since you have no college degree. The Army Air Corps only wants good men who have a college degree," adding "and if you don't make real good grades in school you don't stand a ghost of a chance. What kind of grades do you make?" Before I could get a chance to answer, he continues, "By the way, what kind of physical shape are you in?

Furthermore if I were in charge, you would be advised that there is absolutely no way you would make it."

I could only take a half hour of this overbearing, swaggering Major uncle of mine, when I said: "Sorry I took so much of your valuable time, Sir! *but I am going to be a pilot.*"

With a cool but polite voice he ushered me out of his house with, "That's fine, Son, Good-bye." Down deep I felt there must be another way.

A couple of years passed when the U.S. became embroiled in the war. With the help of several men in the Lion's Club, a study group was formed to help kids like me prepare to take the competitive exam in lieu of the college requirements. The regulations for cadets said that if a person lacked the college requirements a waiver would be issued if he passed the competitive exam for the Aviation Cadets, however he must make a grade of 75% or higher and pass a very rigid flight physical.

My next big step was how to get my folks to sign the waiver to let me in. I was just 18, but anyone under 21 was required to have both parent's signatures before he could even hope to take the written exam.

I had a hard job trying to convince my folks that I wanted to fly. My Dad wouldn't sign the waiver unless my Mom did. My Mom wouldn't sign unless my Dad did. It was a Mexican stand-off. For over two weeks I tried every way I knew to get the waiver signed, with absolutely no luck.

Then a light dawned. Maybe this might work, I thought. I went to my Mom and said, "Dad would sign if you signed, but he really did not want to be the first to sign it."

"OK," Mom said, as she signed the paper. Next I went to my Dad and said, "See, Mom signed, now you can." Boy, that's easy, I thought. Less than a week later my parents, comparing notes, found out how their son had duped them. It was a bit touchy for a while, but when they realized how serious I was about this flying, they agreed it would be OK for me to go into the Aviation Cadets.

With the legal paper work out of the way, I really went to work in preparation for taking the written test. I spent every available evening that I could studying. Oh, how I wished I had studied harder while I was in school.

No matter, I felt that with this extra help from the men in the Lions Club, I would stand a better chance to make it. I guess down deep I can still hear my Uncle saying, "There is no way, absolutely no way without your degree." Could he be right?

The men helping us kept reminding me not to give up. Taking the train to lower Manhattan, N.Y., I had to admit, I was scared. I felt deep down I could pass, but not knowing what to expect left me uptight.

The dream almost became a nightmare as I flipped over page after page of this exam. I couldn't believe the questions that were asked. Sure, we did prepare for this, but I felt that it was a lot harder than we were led to believe.

It was an all-day exam, and at the conclusion we all compared notes. At this point, none of us felt that he had a chance. We had been advised that if we passed, we would be notified and advised when to come back for our flight physical. The waiting was the hardest part. It took about two weeks, and finally the long awaited letter. "You are to report for your flight physical. . . ."

It was one hell of a physical. I have never had one like it before. Comparing notes with my buddies, I found that I was the only one of our gang that managed to pass both written and physical exams. I had to wait several months before I got the word to leave for flight training. Finally I was told to report to Kelly Field, San Antonio, Texas.

This was a dream come true. Oh, how badly I wanted to see my Uncle, Major Weeks, and tell him, "*See, I told you I could make it.*" I still did not have my Silver Wings and it would take over a year before I would be able to say, "I told you so."

The 18 passenger Curtiss Condor similar to the ones that used to fly daily from New York to Boston.
(Photo courtesy McDonnell Douglas Corp.)

Introduction to dive bombing with the A-24, the Army's version of the Navy's dive bomber called the "Dauntless".
(Photo courtesy Aero Graphics.)

Chapter 2
World War II Flight Training

Word finally arrived and I was ordered to report to down-town New York City for the troop train ride to Kelly Field, San Antonio, Texas and flight training. This modern version of travel was a belching steam engine roaring and raring to go. It was pulling about 25 Pullman cars.

Most of the time we had no idea where we were. Stopping for water or switching train crews, we constantly asked the neighbors, "Where are we?" Even when they told us, we still had to ask, "But what state?" They were astonished to think that we were so dumb.

The train went up the Hudson Valley then through western Canada and across the beautiful mountains. Our next known area was the twin cities of Minneapolis, St. Paul, Minn. Now down through the Dakotas, Oklahoma City, and finally San Antonio, Texas, five days later.

Arriving at Kelly Field, we checked in. Marching and singing, we went on to the hair cutting shop. Next came the uniforms, shots, and paper work. Physical training was a must and we did an awful lot of running. Of course, the stone brigade made up for what little spare time we had.

Over-head, twin engine C-45's (Twin Beechcrafts) flew day and night. It was truly an exciting time. Finally we got our orders and class assignment. We were now known as the Class of 43-B. Going by bus to Primary flight school at Coleman, Texas, was a real trip. Hot, dry and dusty.

Starting out in elements of five, little did we think that the wash-out rate would be so high. Three out of five, and even as high as four out of five was not uncommon. It was here in flight school that I acquired the nickname of "Doc," in due reverence to the famous comic strip character Doc Savage that was playing in all of the newspapers at that time.

We had all types of civilian instructors and each one had his own techniques. My particular instructor had the habit of rapidly moving the stick left and right beating me on my knees to make sure I would get the point and do it right. My knees were so sore that there were times when I could hardly crawl up on the wing of the ship. I was ready to kill him a few times but I had to admit he did dramatically get across his points.

Another instructor had a horrible habit of moving the stick rapidly forward and then back, this always helped get a student's attention. One day for some unknown reason his student may not have had his belt fastened, or may have accidentally loosened his seat belt. At any rate, with the last pop of the stick, the instructor watched in shock as Cadet Reynolds went flying out of the cockpit in free flight.

Hours later, Reynolds was found in a field dead, chute un-opened. That brought to an end this particular type of instruction.

It was real hot this particular day and the usual procedure after a flight was a cold Coke, a Clark candy bar and a cigarette. I had just finished my Coke when Jim Robertson came up to me and said, "Hey Doc, want a Coke?" "Gee, I just finished one, but I guess I can handle another," I said.

"Great, how about two, or three?" said Jim.

"What gives?" I said, looking at him in disbelief as most of the cadets were always short on money.

"Apparently the machine is stuck and is giving out free Cokes," said Jim in response. "Step right up, fellows, drinks are on the house." We all had our fill and then some. Little did we realize the dire consequences that were about to take place. We all would pay and pay dearly.

The next day the Colonel came storming out to our formation and told us that, as a result of the money theft from the Coke machine, the honor of the Cadet Corps was at stake unless the guilty party came forth.

"How can the guilty party come forth?" we asked each other.

Tomorrow was Saturday and all leaves were cancelled, but so what. The Colonel was bound and determined to sweat it out of us. He had the complete class report out on the airport ramp in full dress uniforms with parachutes strapped on our backs. We were ordered to march on the ramp

A-24 Army version of the Navy Douglas Dauntless. Dive brakes opened and starting dive. (Photo courtesy U.S. Air Force Museum.)

for over three hours in the hot sun. Still no results. We were exhausted, unable and unwilling to turn anyone in to save the cadets honor code. There was just no possible way we could. The Colonel seeing that this produced no results finally called it to a halt before some one got hurt.

Basic at Goodfellow Field, San Angelo, Texas, did not produce as many wash-outs, but we did lose six pilots in fatal accidents. A mystery then, but now the cause is readily identified as vertigo. Several pilots flying at night reaching down for a map or to change a gas selector valve, fell victim to this.

At Advanced Flying School in Eagle Pass, Texas, we were just about assured of our silver wings, unless of course, we screwed up too badly. Upon graduation in February 1943, we all had a wide choice of assignments. I really wanted to be a fighter pilot.

The volunteer assignment lists read as follows:

Ten slots open for P-40's
Five slots open for P-39's (Wow, this is my first choice).

Other slots open were for the Training Command, Transport Command, and one with a strange twist, Dive-Bomber.

My mouth watered as I contemplated these choice assignments. We were given the opportunity to list our preferences. But who the hell in their right mind would want to be a dive-bomber pilot? Looking closer at this assignment was an extra line added to this description: 30 DAYS LEAVE!

"Red" Sandler, my old buddy said, "Hey Doc, let's put this one first, everyone will want it because of the leave. Then we will pick the fighter plane P-39 second and the P-40 third. I'll bet you we will get the fighters because everyone will want the time off to go home."

"Sounds good to me," I said. We got our orders and both Red and I were shocked as we read them. We had been assigned to the dive-bomber school at Key Field, Meridian, Mississippi. After thirty days leave, we were ordered to report to Key Field. "God, what the hell kind of a dumb choice did we make?" I chided Red.

Arriving at the 48th Dive Bombing Group, we found the Army Air Corps was actually flying A-24's. The Navy Douglass Dauntless. It was almost like an overgrown AT-6. It was a slow airplane but it did have the perforated-cheese dive brakes that initiated us into dive bombing. We were truly amazed to find everything ass-backwards on this ship.

"Why the Navy did this, I don't know," I told Red. On every take-off you had to change hands to use the gear, flaps or dive-brakes. As far as we were concerned, the throttle on the right side meant you had to change hands every time to do anything.

We were training for short field take-offs and landings. Strange, but we couldn't shake the feeling we were being trained for carrier flying. It was just a few months later we learned of the Army Air Corps fighter pilots taking off from a carrier and landing on the Casablanca beachhead.

Within a couple of months we were switched to flying the A-31 (Vultee Vengeance) and then the A-35 (Vultee Vangard). The Army Air Corps version of the Dive Bomber were real hunks of junk. In five flights with the A-35, I had one in-flight fire and had to make an emergency landing at Birmingham, Alabama. The other two were more fright flights. We hated these ships with a passion.

Both Red and I were constantly bitching at each other for being so damn foolish for picking this assignment. We were pretty bitter when suddenly orders were cut for us to report to Baton Rouge, Louisiana, to fly the North American A-36 Dive-Bomber. This was the fore-runner to the P-51 Mustang. Life took on a new meaning and for the first time since graduation I really looked forward to flying a great airplane with the Army Air Corps.

The Army Air Corps Vultee dive-bomber. Used in training at Key Field, Meridian, Mississippi. (Photo courtesy U.S. Air Force Museum.)

Chapter 3
"Beaumont Radio, I Have A Problem"

This night was to be special. Orders had been given for the first formation flight at night. It was to be one of the training missions that made up a new pilot's Form 5, and was in preparation for the ultimate goal, that of a fully trained fighter pilot ready for combat.

It was supposed to be a two-ship mission, with each pilot taking a turn at leading and navigating every other leg of the cross-country trip. We also had the opportunity to pick who we wanted to fly with, which in itself was a bit unusual, but nice.

Don Wenger was a very good friend of mine, and he beat me to the punch when he asked me to fly with him. I was quite pleased as we both had flown together before. I eagerly looked forward to this night formation cross-country triangle flight.

We had unofficially flown together a few weeks ago on another cross-country flight that we did not want any one to know about. In fact, it was a real hell-raising flight, and done at night. We both decided that, one at a time, we would buzz the main highway leading from Shreveport, La., to Beaumont, Texas. The main route from Baton Rouge, La., to Beaumont, Tex., was a very long section of highway that ran for many miles just as straight as a die.

We watched for our opportunity to scare the hell out of the motorists. Just as an oncoming car came into view we dove down without any lights

15

leveled off a few feet above the road, and turned on our two main landing lights. This startled the driver and he wound up doing all kinds of wild gyrations. We both chuckled about this later.

Now we knew that this time we had a different role to play. This night formation called for thorough planning on our part, since it meant that we had to change command on each leg of the trip. We flipped a coin for the first leg, and I won the toss. My choice was to lead the first leg. Our trip called for a round robin triangle flight. From Baton Rouge, Shreveport, and back to Baton Rouge. A bit over two hours of night formation flying.

Flight plans all filed and checked, we were cleared to take off on the first leg of the flight. It was another clear night and both of us were looking forward to a nice trip. About half way to Beaumont, Don called and asked me how I was doing. "Fine, no problems, we're right on course," I replied. It was just about this time that I thought my oil temperature was indicating a bit high. I radioed Don and told him about this.

Flying on a bit further, there was no doubt now, the oil temp and the coolant temperatures were both rising. I began to get a bit concerned and had visions of bailing out in the middle of the night to nowhere. We were flying at 10,000 ft., and anxiously I called Don again to advise him of my condition. He was as concerned as I, as we had no real airports nearby. Things indeed looked black.

Scanning my charts, I found a frequency for the Beaumont Airways Communications Station. Dialing up this frequency, I tried to call them in a very calm voice. *"Beaumont Radio . . . This is Air Force 437 calling . . . I have a problem and I may have to bail out."*

"Roger Air Force 437, what is the nature of your problem?"

"I believe that I have an overheating engine and don't know how long it will keep running," I replied.

"Don't worry, we are here to help you any way that we possibly can, just don't bail out. We can get you to an airport where you can land safely."

"That's great," I replied, "But where?"

"Right here," the voice answered. I thought for a minute and just did not remember any airport near there. Neither did Don.

They must have been reading our minds, as they came back and advised, "This strip here at our station is large enough. A ship similar to yours landed here less than a month ago," they said.

"Are you sure it was an A-36?" I asked.

"Exactly," they replied.

That did it and I felt that I should be able to land there without a bit of trouble. Requesting that they turn on the lights, I heard them come back with a "Roger, we will have the lights on the field for you." This sounded a bit strange. What did they mean? *Lights on the field.*

I told them I would make a pass first to make sure everything was OK. Don was now tucked tightly in next to me as I made a low pass over the field. I still did not know from one minute to the next whether the engine would seize up and quit.

Don encouraged me by saying, "Doc, I think it would be better to try and land, rather than bail out at night."

"I certainly agree with you Don," I said, "I'll go for it." Don stayed up high circling and watched me as I made the final preparation for the landing. Flaps, gear, and gas selector. Boy, those lights sure looked dim, I thought. Eight lights lined up at the end of the runway. Another set of eight lights are at the far end of the runway. When . . . *Holy Cow!* I suddenly realized *they're cars parked at each end of the runway with their lights on.*

Now with horror, I notice a high tension line directly in the path of my ship's landing lights. "*DAMN* . . . why now," I think. Pulling up, I narrowly missed them. I am just about over the car's lights as my left eye catches the top of the cars. I barely clear them by inches. As I level off and land a loud clatter, then a tremendous roar greets me. I just don't know what is happening. It sounded like several machine guns banging away at me. I felt like I had gotten to the end of the runway awful fast as the lights from the cars loomed up directly in front of me.

Don radioed down to me, "Well done Doc! I'll go on back to the base and let the C.O. know what happened."

Taxiing back, I still heard this same clanking sound. My two lights pointed the way to several guys waving at me to park by their building. I pivoted on one wheel using my brake and immediately dug a big hole in the ground. It was just physically impossible to move it anymore. Shutting down, I hopped out and received a host of congratulations from all the crowds of people who had gathered around both to help and watch the show.

I then noticed that the runway was made up of oyster shells. One of the guys advised me that the whole runway was like this, including the parking area. Even though the ground was wet, it did support me until I tried to turn. They were all very happy that I got down safe and I thanked them for helping get so many people out this hour of the night to help me.

"By the way," one guy asked, "Just what kind of an airplane is that you're flying?"

"An A-36," I answered.

"Boy, that's the largest fighter plane that we have ever seen in here," he replied.

"I don't get it, I thought you told me you had a fighter like this land here before?"

"*Naw . . . not like this . . .* our airport is only 3,000 ft. long and they were two place Army fighter planes."

TWO PLACE?" I said.

"Yup, it was a two place airplane."

"You mean a two place trainer, don't you?" I said.

"Yeah, I guess so," he replied in a bewildered voice as he looked in awe at this huge fighter that had just landed at this little Piper Cub field.

For tonight only, it suddenly turned into an airport that was barely big enough for this awesome Army Air Corps fighter plane.

The A-36 Dive Bomber similar to the used on the night flight of the story from *"Beaumont Radio."*
(Photo courtesy North American/Rockwell Corp.)

Chapter 4
Rock-N-Roll

The advanced flight training program was rapidly drawing to a close. We all knew it wouldn't be too long before we would be bound for one of the theaters of war. We had no idea whether it would be Europe or Asia.

I believe if we had our choice, it would be Europe, but it wasn't for us to choose. We still had to complete a few more live firing missions, both air and ground. This one day was scheduled for a ground attack mission on a set up target located east of Baton Rouge, Louisiana. Occasionally we had targets set up in Lake Pontchartrain. It was fun to see the bullets kick up all the water as the pilots tried to put as many holes as they could into the target.

A few of the pilots still lacked the total qualifications requirements and this was one of those days that they were required to make it up. We also had to take our turn on the range as the duty officer. I did not look forward to this duty as it meant a long jeep ride out to the range and back.

It was my turn to pull ground observation Officer-Of-The-Day duty and personally I did not relish this assignment. It generally meant a before dawn ride, cramped quarters, missed lunch and a lot of other problems, including increased paper work. Incidentally it was quite noisy, and there was some danger involved. Not critical, but one had to be careful.

The first flight of four A-36's radioed our position and advised that they were about ready to begin their strafing attack. No question about it, excitement ran high as the pilots flew overhead and began their long steep glide down towards the ground target firing all six machine guns. After the dust and smoke settled, the targets were marked and made ready for the next group.

The next group of four lined up and started down, "Not bad shooting," I remarked to the Sergeant next to me as the last ship came in just blazing away for all he was worth.

"Damn, he is getting awful close to the target," I said.

Then, "*Oh No! . . . No! . . .*" The ship hit the target in a forty-five degree angle. It was a sad thing to watch helplessly as a fellow pilot just ended it all. Reporting back to base we notified headquarters how we watched a pilot get "*target fixation*" and then slam into the ground.

Shortly thereafter, we got our orders to ship out. We got all the required shots, Tetanus, Small-Pox, Typhoid, Malaria, etc. Now since we got those Malaria shots, does this mean that we will be going to the Far East?

Packed up on a train, we were off. But to where? Seventeen of us arrived at Norfolk, Va., and were told nothing, except that we were to be going overseas. Many hours were spent in train stations or at whistle stops waiting for crews or trains, coal, water or whatever. We never really got used to the idea of wasting so much time. This trip was also no exception. While in the train station word came that we would be here for at least three more hours. "Oh God, not again," I moaned.

Getting off our car I walked up to this huge steam engine on the track next to our troop train that was puffing and belching smoke and steam and not going anywhere. I waved to the Engineer and Fireman and they waved back. Next thing I knew the engineer beckoned me to come on board. I think it might have been my uniform, or probably the shiny silver wings that caught the engineer and crew's attention. At any rate I was thrilled to be invited aboard.

Eagerly climbing up the steps I was awed by the noise, gadgets and friendliness of the crew. I asked all kinds of questions and finally said to the Engineer, "Boy, I have always wanted to drive one of these steam engines."

"I know, son," said the Engineer, "but it will just have to be a dream."

"But, I'm going to war as a Fighter Pilot and I might never ever get another chance," I said. Well, that did it.

"Get up in my seat, boy," said the engineer. "Here is the throttle, brakes, and whistle. Give it three blasts and let's go up the track." WOW! I was speechless as we huffed and puffed up the track past our stalled troop train. Blowing the whistle, I waved wildly at my buddies. I was now the envy of the whole gang. All too soon I had to come back to our place of reality, as I drove the steam engine back. I thanked the engineer and crew and wondered what they really thought of this nervy young pilot kid who just promoted this ride.

Now we started boarding our boat, the Colin P. Kelly, a brand new Liberty ship. How appropriate, I thought. This ship had been named after our first Army Air Corps B-17 pilot hero.

We were soon at sea with over 200 other ships that made up our huge convoy. Rather comforting knowing that we had a better chance with so large a convoy. We felt much more secure as we watched our little destroyer escorts known as, "The Greyhounds of the Sea," offering their alertness and protection while they constantly circled our ships. In addition, we had a "Baby Flat Top" that carried four little Navy planes they circled over us during the daylight hours, always constantly alert for enemy subs. About one week out the shit hit the fan. We ran into unbelievably foul weather. All of our dishes were broken the first hour. This meant we would eat from mess kits from now on. We had 1800 paratroopers along with 17 pilots. The bunks were 10 high and as soon as one of the soldiers on the top got sick, puking down the bunks, others followed in turn.

It was a mess, but none of the pilots got sick, yet it was a wonder they didn't. The crew of the ship loved it, because this meant less chance of a sub attack in this bad weather. Looking out over the rocking rolling ship, I am truly flabbergasted. I thought we were alone but now you see the whole fleet as we top out on a huge wave. Other ships were visible and several had started down the waves and I thought, "My God, the ships looked like they were all about to sink." The propellor screws were completely out of the water as it dove down, nose first, into its watery grave.

Now our turn comes and, *"Oh No, we're not going to make it!"* I yell to the guy next to me as we dive down into the huge watery hole. Struggling up the far side, the wall of water now starts covering the bow and engulfs the ship. It feels like we are almost completely underwater.

We got thoroughly soaked as we hung on for our lives to the safety rope line tied next to the cabins. After three more fanatic pitches, I said to

Frank Davis, "Enough of this, I can't stand to watch us almost sink," and I went below.

The nights were beautiful after we left the storm, but the full moon made us very concerned. It presented a good target for any sub that might be lurking nearby. We generally made it a point to play cards all night. We all felt that there was absolutely no way that we would ever want to be trapped below decks asleep, if we were attacked. So usually we slept on deck in the day and stayed up all night.

The constant POW . . . POW . . . POW of the engine was monotonous, but the day it stopped really got our attention. We nervously watched as the convoy sailed on. They never waited up for any stragglers. We were on our own. Marooned out here alone, we were a sitting duck. The little airplanes kept us constant company which was some consolation.

Late that afternoon, the ship's crew finally repaired our problem and it was indeed comforting to hear the booming of the engine again. The ship quivered and groaned as the Captain gave it full power trying to catch up with the convoy. Later that night we finally did manage to pick up the ships and join them in a tail-end charley position.

We had one hell-of-a-scare a few days later when the Greyhounds began whooping it up, whistling and starting to drop depth charges all over the place. Finally it was all quiet again and we proceeded to do our usual zig-zag type of trip. Beyond any doubt, I'm sure we must have added an extra four or five days to our trip because of the constant zig-zagging, 24 hours a day.

Early one morning we woke up to a complete silence. *"Oh, not again!"* I say to several of the guys next to me.

It was daylight and we were rocking back and forth ever so gently. We started checking with the ship's crew to see just what-in-hell was happening now. "Why absolutely nothing," they said, as we all looked out over the bay to a beautiful white city on the horizon.

Despite this beautiful city, we were surrounded by hundreds of little boats, rafts, almost anything imaginable that floats. Each had several dirty ragged bearded men begging for coins. Their vessels were not very seaworthy as they were listing to the point of almost capsizing. We threw a few coins out to them and they immediately dove overboard, clothes and all. A few seconds later they emerged spewing water and smiling with the money clutched between their teeth.

"Must be the rift-raft of the city," I remarked to Roland Tapp. We reached land a few hours later. Everyone in the city looked like the men in the boats.

"Well, after 25 days at sea, can you guys finally tell us just where in hell we are now?" I asked a couple of Merchant Marine sailors standing next to me at the ship's rail.

"You bet," he replied, "We're in Casablanca."

"Just where in hell is that?" I ask.

"Why, North Africa," he replied.

A group of pickled P-47's arriving from the States on the aircraft carrier located in Casablanca North Africa. Will soon be ready for combat.
(Photo courtesy Savage collection.)

Two German 110's, typical of the types used against the Allies in Italy, 1943. (Photo courtesy U.S. Air Force Museum)

Chapter 5
The Salerno Beachhead

Unpacking at Casablanca, we savored the sights and smells of the city. We were not prepared for what we saw. Natives in long dirty white robes. Dirty beards and flies all over everything. It was almost impossible to keep them off you. I can understand why. The natives were often seen squatting on the street as they relieved themselves right out in the open. No one seemed to care.

We only stayed in Casablanca a couple of nights. We soon found our group on a C-47 (a military version of the DC-3) flying on to Oran, North Africa. Here we spent another five days. From Oran we flew on to Algiers and landed in a blinding dust storm. We were to taste and grind sand in our mouths for the next three days. The desert storm finally blew itself out and we were on our way to the front.

Again we stopped. This time in Tunis. It seemed like we would never get to our combat outfit. Another week and we were on our way once again flying in the C-47 up to the coast of Italy.

After more than a month of traveling, using various means of transportation, trains, trucks, boat, and air, we finally arrived on the Salerno Beachhead in Italy.

The airport strip was a beehive of activity. It was good just to see airplanes flying again. We were all assigned our Squadrons and our motel accommodations (five men in a tent). I met my new group of tent-mate pilots; Broderick, Sammonds, Schofield and Enchenlaub. In such close quarters, we soon got to know each other quite intimately. For the first time in my career, I let myself get close to these guys in the tent. Too close really. We lived, fought, drank, swore, played cards, etc. We were like one.

Within two days after checking in, we met our Group Commander and our operations boss. He knew that we all had been grounded for a long time, not because we wanted to, it just took us over a month to get here from the States.

Checking out our flying gear, we were each next introduced to our Chief Mechanic and Armament Officer. There was a lot to learn before we could go out on a combat mission. After the formal introduction and welcome, the CO then said, "All of you are to check out a ship and get current. Remember, when you fly here, fly south. We still have the Germans about 40 or so miles north of us. Now go out, have fun and get yourself reacquainted with our airplanes. By the way, I expect all of you to go out and do about a half dozen or so vertical dives using the dive brakes." We had dive brakes on our stateside ships, but never used them. Why, I don't know.

It felt good again to savor all of the sights and sounds, including the smell of gasoline and engine fumes of a real military airport. Being on a boat out in the Atlantic was not our idea of military.

Checking out my gear, I was soon down on the strip ready for my first flight in over 40 days. That's the longest I had gone without flying since my solo flight in the Air Corps.

Taking off, I was electrified again with the performance of this magnificent fighter. After three touch-and-go landings, I started climbing up to 12,000 feet in preparation for my first true vertical dive. Carefully checking out the area below, I mentally got set for the dive.

Opening the brakes, I felt the ship start to shudder and I had a chill in anticipation of what was about to transpire. Rolling over on my back, I sucked the stick to my stomach, and started down . . . *Straight down!*

Both feet are standing flat on the rudder pedals and my whole body was being held back by the shoulder straps. Why it's incredible . . . I'm looking at the ground as I have never seen it before. I thought, "Man, now this is a piece of cake." I felt great and I began pulling out of the 350 MPH vertical dive about 5,000 feet above the ground, then I closed the brakes to start my recovery.

When . . . *POW!* I felt like someone in the cockpit hit me in the back of the head with a baseball bat. I saw stars.

Recovering from this bizarre effect, I returned to the field. Reporting to my CO, I explained, "Sir, I doubt seriously if I could ever dive again."

"Nonsense," said the Colonel, "go out and do a few more." Reluctantly, I agreed. He was right, three more dives and I felt right at home.

Our ships had been out on sorties and our strip was noisily busy with the normal everyday activity. It was clear and fairly warm. I was out of my tent making the usual preparations for the morning chores. My helmet served as the bathroom sink and tub. I had just brushed my teeth and bathed. New water was added and once again the little Sterno like Bunsen burner was set up under the helmet to heat the water. My face was completely lathered and I was ready to start the shaving process. Suddenly overhead about 9,000, an A-36 came zooming up over the field. Nothing too exciting but we always had to look up as she screamed by.

I had just about completed three strokes with the razor when I heard the engine starting to miss a few beats. In fact, the whole camp came to an almost eerie silence as the ship started backfiring and blowing out white smoke . . .

Then the engine quit. Now all you could hear was the shrill scream from the sick ship. The scream was always present from the dive brakes, but today was different. It was now almost like a death scream due to the dead engine.

There were several guys standing around me, and all I could say was, "*BAIL OUT! . . . BAIL OUT!! PLEASE*," but they replied, "Aw, hell, he will make it, he is right over the field."

I sensed doom as he kept his nose so high in the turns. He had just completed one full turn with quite a bit of altitude left, when he started another turn.

He kept a constant turn to the left, his nose was still way too high. I kept saying over and over again, "Please get your nose down . . . *bail out!*"

He had just about completed the second full 360 degree left turn and was almost ready to start his final roll-out to the runway. As he started the roll-out turn, the ship tucked under and went into a left turn spin. It hit the dirt runway in a nose-down, left wing-down attitude, and then wound up doing a couple of cartwheels. Each time a part of the ship hit the ground, pieces came flying off. On first impact there was a huge explosion that rocked our whole area.

Almost immediately, the first explosion was followed by a series of smaller ones as the live ammo began to light off. We all ducked for cover. In about an hour most of the fireworks had calmed down and it was safe enough to stick our heads out. The soap on my face had dried and I had forgotten all about it, until one smart ass said, "Boy, do you look a sight."

We had found out later that this luckless pilot had just transferred from a local P-40 group. They had been used to flying their ships this way, slow and nose high. It was his first check out ride in the A-36. The accident was firmly planted in my mind and even to this day, I can still see this guy in panic, trying to make it.

It was a short time later that I was faced with a similar situation in, "A Unique Airport."

Word had been received that a new movie from the states was due to be shown at the Air Force movie house in Salerno. Gathering a group of movie buffs together, I checked out a command car. This vehicle usually holds six men, but on this trip tonight we had eight pilots squeezed in.

The drive was only about 10 miles, but driving this truck with the headlights covered was tough because of the blackout regulations. Both head lights were covered completely except for small slits.

There was no way you could safely drive faster than 15-20 MPH.

Prior to our leaving, we picked up some booze to tide us over for the dry spell. The movie was not very good and the boys decided maybe it would be more fun just to get drunk. "Why not?" one guy said. "We need to relax."

I thought that I could hold my liquor, but found out all too soon that it was no contest for me.

It was close to midnight as we started back to the base. Everyone wanted to get back quickly and the pressure was on me to drive fast. In my present condition, I really did not need much help as my foot obeyed their every command.

"Let's go faster," came the orders from several very intoxicated voices. Speeding and bouncing down the dirt road, black-out lights on and trying to pick my way through the bombed out holes, made for a very interesting trip.

Suddenly one of the guys yells, *"Look out for that big hole!"*

"What big hole?" I shout back, as we hit it full tilt. We went flying in the air and finally came down with one big *WACK!* . . . No big deal, at least, we are all in one piece, I think. Further down the road, we go through the very same procedure, again more shouting and laughing.

One of the guys in the back starts singing, "Oh, I'm singing in the rain, singing in the rain." Another guy says, "Hey, that's great singing, but why that song?"

"Why?" becaush! It's raining, that's why," came the reply.

"You're nuts, and drunk," says another pilot.

"No, I'm not that drunk, it really is raining, I can feel it on my head."

At his insistence, I stop the command car and despite my general condition found a flashlight and shined it on this guy's head and face. "My God!" said one of the guys, "he is full of blood." Blood was gushing out of the top of his head all over his face, ears, and down on his uniform. It was that last bump that did him in. He went flying up and hit his head on the metal bar that supported the canvas roof. We used up all of our handkerchiefs trying to stem the flow of blood.

"Look, Doc," said Davis, "It's no use. We can't stop the bleeding, we have to get him to a first aid station." We finally found a medical aid station open down the road and checked him in. In our present condition, everyone in the car thought this was a pretty hilarious situation. The doctor, a Major, met us in the tent.

He had been asleep and was not in a very good mood.

"Which one of you pilots was driving?" he asked.

"Ha, Ha, me, Sir," I replied, after saluting him.

"I don't think this is so very funny, Lieutenant, and as for the rest of you happy fly-boys, it's time to come to your senses and sober up. In fact, we are very short-handed here and I will need help. You all can stay here and see just what has to be done." Handing us towels and a battery-powered light, he ushered us into a large medical tent.

Believe me, that did the job as we watched the doctor start to wash the wound and begin sewing it up, stitch by stitch. After the third stitch, I felt my legs turning to rubber, I just had to get out of there fast for fresh air. I was not alone. The doctor made his point, but he was still quite angry for that unnecessary late office call.

We drove home in silence and wondered how to explain all the blood that now completely covered the back seat of the car. Hell, this was all part of war.

After a dozen or so missions, we had one mission posted for Cassino. No one ever looked forward to this mission. I was lucky. I missed this particular one because I wasn't scheduled. As the Squadron returned, we looked up and as usual automatically started counting the returning five elements. One . . . two . . . three . . . two missing.

Then I hear a guy gasp, "*OH MY GOD! Only one ship left in this ele-ment.*" Now the last ship is in and accounted for. After they landed, we rushed down to operations inquiring as to what element lost all the ships.

They had been flying up a valley that was supposed to be clear of flak. Unknown to them, the Germans had moved in mobile flak trains and units on both sides of the valley. It was bedlam. My friends and buddies were in the first element and caught the worst of it. Sammonds, Schofield, Eichen-laub, were all shot down. It was a black day for Broderick and me in our now almost empty five man tent.

Bob Barnett decked out and ready to go in his A-36.
(Photo courtesy Bob Barnett.)

Savage departing on a mission out of the Salerno beachhead airport. Note: dive brakes in the open position. The crew chief rode on wing to help guide the pilot when he taxies. (Photo courtesy Savage collection.)

Chapter 6
Come Watch The Show

It was one of those days when everything seemed to go just right. In fact, this particular mission started late in the afternoon, which in itself was a bit unusual, as most of the trips were scheduled for early morning.

Target for this afternoon was again the Anzio Beachhead, a dive-bomb attack against an artillery position, and then proceed on inland and north to a German airfield.

After our dive-bomb attack we proceeded to the airfield. First pass on the airfield torched six ships on the ground. It was a complete surprise and it made for a picture perfect mission. I personally saw my guns set fire to a He-111 that was parked on the ramp. Pulling away from the carnage, we all felt quite fortunate that no one took a hit.

Regrouping, we headed for home. The usual right echelon low level approach and peel-up signified that we were home and safe. My turn came and I made the pitch-up to the left with a half roll. While on my back, I lowered the flaps and gear simultaneously. Looking down at the gear lights, I waited for the usual three green lights to come on indicating that all three were down and locked, and safe to land.

Surprise! . . . two red and one green. The green light was the down tail wheel indication. "Could be a malfunction," I thought. I tried pulling the throttle back but only got the gear warning horn in response. I had to abort and let the rest of the Squadron come in behind me. After they all had landed, I then called the tower for permission to make a low pass and a visual check on my gear.

"Tailwheel down, gear doors open, main wheels up," came the reply. This just confirmed what I already knew.

The radio crackled my call sign again, and the voice of the Maintenance Officer suggested, "Have you gone through the emergency procedures completely?"

"Roger, I did all that," I replied, "but still negative on the gear."

"Then go up high and try shaking them down," came his next order.

"OK," I replied, but after complying with his request, I came back with, "Still negative on the gear, sir."

My Base Commander was on the radio now and advised . . . "Circle up higher and overhead until most of your fuel is exhausted." I climbed up higher and watched with some amusement the swelling crowd of curious, as the trucks, emergency vehicles, and people lined up on each side of the runway waiting for the show to begin. It was starting to get dark now, and I called on the radio, "Request permission to make the landing."

"How much fuel do you have left?" came the response.

"About a little less than a quarter in each tank," I replied.

"Roger, that's great, *Good Luck!*"

"Boy . . . those guys are something else," I think, "all lined up to watch the show, and *I am the show.*"

I made a wide circle out over the Salerno Bay and turned to the southwest on my down-wind leg. Dropping the flaps, I made my turn to the base leg. The mountains were now behind me as I prepared for the final approach to landing. With the combination of the ship's camouflage, dark mountains, and twilight, I now disappeared from everyone's view.

Just about this time, the engine coughed once and quit. I had enough altitude to put my nose down and pick a spot to land. I kept telling myself, "keep calm, relax," as the ship gently eased to the ground, tail wheel first. Boy, it was smooth, then . . . *BAM!* . . . the ship hit and the prop came flying off.

Funny, what things enter our mind at a time like this. I thought, "*Boy, that's pretty neat watching the prop snap off and do about a half dozen cartwheels in front of the ship.*"

I sat in the cockpit patting myself on the back issuing congratulations on my surviving. It was about this time I realized that maybe I wouldn't survive, as I was now on a runaway sled, with absolutely no control.

The ship touched down about 100 MPH and was sliding on its belly in the mud. It seemed like it was picking up speed rather than slowing down. The stick and rudder were now completely useless as the ship rapidly began to shift its position and started to slide sideways, left wing first towards a large dirt embankment.

I was now a reluctant passenger frantically staring in utter disbelief, as the ship, skidding sideways, hit the dirt bank with a sickening thud.

The next thing I knew, I was looking up at a huge dirt wall. The A-36 had buried its left wing and engine completely. Shaking off the cobwebs, I loosened my shoulder harness, seat belt, and chute straps. Boy it felt good to know I had survived.

Reaching for the canopy release, I pulled the latch, but to no avail. Next, the emergency release . . . still no go. What a horrible feeling . . . *I'm trapped!*

I know it won't burn, since better than half of the ship is buried in the hill. What to do? I decided that I have to get out now . . . squirming out of my gear, I managed to put my neck, head and shoulders on the seat and parachute. Now with my feet planted against the top of the canopy, I push with all my strength. The canopy finally gives with a loud bang.

Crawling out on the right wing, half dazed, I jump back in fear, as less than two feet away lay a huge coiled snake. The crash has dislodged it from the den. Fortunately, it was in hibernation, as it did not even stir. Sidestepping this obstruction I then noticed about a half dozen "Ities" (Italians) standing on the top of the dike watching me. I must have been out for a while. We were told over and over again, "Whatever you do, don't leave your ship, it's too easy for them (natives) to strip it."

It was almost completely dark now. A couple of the men tried to communicate with me. They spoke no English, so it was a few tense moments, and I was a bit concerned, until one guy offered me a small cigar. This kind of broke the tension as I accepted his offer and took a big drag and almost choked to death on the strong smoke.

Laughing uncontrollably, they all started talking at once. I didn't understand a word, but assured them that I was "OK." This they did understand. "OK, OK," came a half dozen replies.

It seemed incredible that no one saw me go down . . . But it's true, no one was coming. Resigning myself to this fact, I decided that it looked like

I probably would be here all night. It was pitch dark and all hopes of rescue were gone. I knew now that I would be here for the rest of the night and it was getting cold.

About a mile to the north, I thought I saw some bobbing lights. They seemed to be drawing steadily closer and closer, when suddenly I heard a faint cry, "*Hello! Hello out there!* . . . Again, and again, along with a blast of the horn.

Can it be true? They really are out there looking for me.

I put my fingers to my mouth and whistled as loud as I could, just like I used to call for my dog, Pal. I thought they heard me as the truck's horn seemed to blow back a response.

Arriving on the scene about ten minutes later, a Sergeant yells: "*I knew it, I knew it, he is down here and alive.*"

A joyous reunion, and now with a properly clad guard on my ship, we were on our way back to the airport and my Squadron. I arrived at the most appropriate time. The Squadron was having a meeting as I made my grand entrance. Mud up to my butt, a bit of blood on my forehead, and chute draped over my shoulder, I greeted the group.

A cry of dismay . . . *Doc! you're supposed to be dead.*"

"*Hell No! I'm still alive, as you can see,*" I replied, and how about giving me back my gear?"

(It was the usual practice that once a guy went down, all articles were dispersed among the Squadron.)

This comment broke up the meeting and we all retired to the bar to celebrate my return back to the land of the living, and we all wound up getting dead-drunk.

Chapter 7
A Unique Airport

Salerno Beachhead . . . Italy . . . Fall 1943

Our A-36's were making almost daily runs against the target known as the Abbey-on-the-Mount in Cassino. The Germans had the area pretty much ringed with flak and it was not a very safe place to go. They were prepared and ready every time we went there. No such thing as surprise. In fact, every time this mission was posted, we all moaned.

My name was on the board again for this mission. Our strip was getting a bit slippery from the recent rains, and it was a bit tough taking off on the muddy runway with our full loads. Many times we did a dipsy-doodle side motion as the ship went sliding first one way and then the other before we got our tails up enough to gain control. It was always interesting with the field in this condition.

Specifically, the mission for the day was another strike against the stalled lines in Cassino. We carried our usual (2) 500 lb. bombs and ammo load. We were to hit a dug-in group of Tiger Tanks, and then go on from there and stop any movement of anything on the roads above Cassino.

We came in at 10,000 ft., opened our brakes and followed the usual procedure in our dive-bomb attacks. From our combat attack formation, we then assembled in a line astern single file for a dive bomb attack on the target. The Leader waggled his wings and all dive brakes were then opened. He rolled over and started his vertical dive, then the rest of the ships followed him in succession.

The flak was so intense we all discussed and cussed it. After the dive and release of our two bombs, we pulled up, closed our brakes, and re-formed on the leaders in our combat front assembly. Flak was extremely heavy and intense, and rather accurate as it exploded almost at our exact same altitude. We all wanted out of there in a hurry. It was like we had shaken a bee-hive box and the bees were out to get us.

About this time, my ship lurched, and I felt like I just took a hit. The engine quit and then started again, but was running very rough. I radioed my situation to Red Leader One, and he advised, "If it quits, bail out."

I came back with "Roger, it's still running, and I would like to try and get back as far as I can."

"Roger, Roger," came the reply, "I'll send a ship back with you for cover."

The Squadron went on as I turned on back to our lines. About this time my wing man came over to join me. It was a good feeling to think, well, at least, I am not alone.

A big thumbs up and a smile greeted me, along with, "You will make it OK, Doc." I looked over to my left and here was Mike Russo flying my wing. I had been on one wild mission with him when he shot down his fourth ship. He later went on to become the first ace of the 27th Group.

Giving me all the encouragement he could, he watched as I struggled to keep my ship in the air. He asked me, "How bad are you hit, Doc?"

"I really don't know," I replied. It was barely running and I did not want to bail out over enemy lines, even though Russo was with me to offer some protection. It wasn't too many months ago that Joe Caparelli (from my home town in New York) bailed out and was shot as he got near the ground.

Russo was really close now, and kept saying, "You'll make it Doc . . . Hang in there . . . you're doing fine." At this time I was not too sure. The engine was beginning to act worse. After what seemed like an eternity, the strip finally came in sight over the hills of Salerno. What a sight. "Maybe, just maybe, I might make it," I thought.

I called in to the make-shift tower we had set up on the strip and requested landing info, with the added remark, "I have a rough running engine, maybe flak damage, don't know how bad, and am not sure I can still make the strip."

"Roger, Roger, understand," came the reply, "You are cleared to land."

For the first time, I breathed a sigh of relief and then prepared to get set up for the landing. I gave Russo the thumbs up and said, "Thanks."

Then he said, "I'll stick with you," as I lowered the gear and flaps. For the first time I felt I had it made.

Just about 700 ft., above the ground, two red flares were shot off in front of me.

GOD . . . I CAN'T BELIEVE THIS IS FOR REAL. WHY? WHY? I pulled up my gear and flaps and started to climb up and left turn out with my sick ship. As I made my left turn I looked in disbelief. Landing in the opposite direction was a flight of P-40's. They too saw the flares and pulled up and made their left turn out.

The tower came back on the air and said, *"Sorry, but we had no choice."*

"Understand," I replied. As I got to about 1200 ft., the engine gave up and quit.

Oh God! . . . what a feeling. I saw this mental picture flash in my mind of the guy getting killed a few months ago because he turned too low. I made up my mind that I would not do the same thing.

Too low now to bail out, I rolled the ship out on a firm heading to the northwest and started down. Directly in front of me was a large field that had a big ditch cut right in the middle of it. It was roughly 25 ft., wide and about as deep. It was one of the large water ditches that had been cut through the fields. As I came down, I knew the ship would stall and drop into this ditch.

I prayed, *"Dear God, please give me enough pressure to help me drop my flaps."* I felt that I would be able to get enough of a "balloon effect" if I dropped the flaps at the last moment. Maybe . . . just maybe . . . it would then give me enough lift to cause me to float over this open ditch.

Waiting as long as possible and at the very last second, I dropped the flaps. I breathed a sigh of relief as I felt the desired effect and just barely floated past the far end of the ditch.

In fact, I found out a few minutes later that the bottom of the scoop had touched down just a scant foot on the other side of the open ditch. Sliding down to a very gentle stop, the prop popped off and the ship skidded to a stop. Could it be, this was getting a little easier? After all, this was the second time I had done this in two weeks.

I opened the canopy and stepped out on my wing, just glad to be alive. I could tell Mike was very happy, but not as much as I, as he waved his hand and wings and almost took my head off with his last pass. I didn't realize how excited I was until I reached inside my shirt pocket for a cigarette. I pulled out one of my pack hardly able to hold my hands still. Now, as I lighted it up with my trusty Zippo, I found out just how shaky I was.

A couple of drags and a soldier with a rifle came up to greet me. Pointing his rifle at me said:

"SIR . . . PUT THAT DAMN CIGARETTE OUT . . . SIR!
THIS IS A LIVE AMMO DUMP!"

WOW . . . I not only put the butt out, but really got nervous as I looked around for the first time.

Directly in front of the ship was a crate labeled: *DANGEROUS . . . EXPLOSIVES . . . !!! 105 MM.*

Off to the left was another large group of boxes labeled, *HAND GRENADES.*

Looking around I can see many other boxes that had the very same kind of markings.

I had a chance to walk back to where I first touched down. I could see where the bottom scoop on the fuselage came within a foot on the far edge of the ditch. Just a few inches shorter and I would have been smashed like an accordian.

Before help finally arrived I thoroughly examined my ship. Strange, I failed to find a single hole. Later checks and investigation proved contaminates were in the fuel lines. At the time we had only 55 metal gallon drums for fueling.

Prior to getting picked up by the Squadron's vehicle, I did have time to consider this thought.

Man, I sure picked one hell of *"A UNIQUE AIRPORT."*

Chapter 8
The Yo . . . Yo . . .

Today dawned bright and beautiful. It was hard to believe that we were really at war. The whole Squadron was up bright and early and as rumor had it, we were about to pull off a very important mission; one that was to be a big help in stemming the flow of materials down to the Germans in the southern part of Italy.

We finished our breakfast shortly after six, and we were told that the briefing would take place at 7 A.M. in the tobacco warehouse. But still there was no word as to where this mission would be.

We all wound up for the briefing shortly before the magic hour, but still not a hint as to where we would be going. Looking over the ready board, I found my name right at the top of the list. The Colonel made it a point not to post names on the board prior to the mission. It usually made it pretty tough to sleep if you had to think about a mission for the next day.

Calling the briefing to order, it was announced that the mission for the day was to be a dive-bomb attack against the rail head of the town of Bologna, Italy, located on the Adriatic Sea.

For once the intelligence sector reported that little or no flak could be expected. That was a joke. They are right so few times, except for the Cassino area, it's no joke.

With take-off time scheduled for 9 A.M., we returned to our area and prepared for the mission. Carrying our chutes and other equipment, we usually got a jeep ride out to the flight line and our ships.

As I settled into my ship, I wondered if this mission would be one of those milk runs that I had heard about but never lucky enough to get one.

Firing up the Allison engine I taxied out to the ready position for departure. The make-shift Tower gave us the green light for take-off and in turn we roared off the dirt strip at Salerno. In no time flat, we had formed up in our usual formation front attack of four ships each. The Group made up the grand total of 16 ships, four to the element. It was very much like the fingers on a hand, excluding the thumb. Flying in this line abrest configuration gave us a lot of flexibility.

Mission for the day was to be a dive-bomb attack against the railroad station of Bologna, Italy, located on the Adriatic Sea. The flight of 16 A-36's made up the Squadron's strength.

Not an all-out striking force, but it did represent a very strong effort. Thirty two five hundred pound bombs would do a lot of damage. We mainly carried two 500 lb. bombs, although once in a while we did carry frag bomb clusters, under our wings. This particular mission called for the very heavy demolition type.

Nearing the target of Bologna, the leader's radio crackled the command, "Line astern in preparation for the dive-bomb attack." All 16 ships obeyed his order and formed up in a line astern. We were now in position for the run. Just about every one of our dive-bomb attacks were started at the 10,000 foot level. The leader waggled his wings, the standard signal for the opening of the dive brakes. The weather was excellent for this time of the year, and surprise . . . very little flak was encountered.

Each ship in turn rolled over on its back and started the vertical dive. Now it's my turn. Peering intently at the target, I used my ring gunsights to line up the railroad yards. Locating the railroad station dead center, I waited for the right time to fire my four machine guns, with the two nose guns held in reserve. Using tracers and incendiaries I lined up the ship's path prior to dropping the bombs.

A vertical dive is quite a sensation. You will actually find yourself going straight down with feet standing flat on the rudder pedals.

Bombs away! and we zoomed back up to rejoin the Squadron. Climbing for altitude, we had to clear the mountains before we could head out for the second phase of our mission, *an armed recon flight.*

The mountains around Bologna station topped the 8,000 foot level. Nearing the top of the mountains we were almost ready to leave the scene when several guys noticed a long column of smoke that marked a freight train puffing up the tracks serenely and completely unaware of the now demolished station.

The Squadron Leader's radio shot out: "Blue one take your element down, and destroy that train!" Acknowledgment was made and four of us immediately dove down towards the puffing, smoking train. We felt pretty confident about this task, after all we now had twelve ships to form our top cover as we carried out that order.

Our first pass sent the engine sky high. Parts went flying in all directions. We were quite fortunate that no parts of this destruction hit us. Next concentrating on the box cars, we slammed hundreds of 50 caliber slugs into several box cars. Four of them blew up almost simultaneously.

A couple of more passes and we pretty much had destroyed the major part of the freight train, including the engine.

Climbing back up to rejoin the Squadron, we felt quite relaxed as we saw our top cover circling overhead. One of the guys called on the radio and said, "Hey, our ships are sure flying pretty sloppy formation today."

"Roger," chimes another, "But wait, they ain't our ships."

"Aw, they're just Spitfires," came another reply.

"It can't be," said the other wingman, "they don't carry enough fuel to be up this far."

Just about this time, three of the ships belch puffs of black smoke.

"Jesus Christ, they're Me-109's. Holy shit, they really have us by the balls . . .!!"

I yelled, "STAY OFF THE AIR." It was just about this time that the gum in my mouth turned to a huge dry cotton ball. My left leg was shaking so bad, I had to hold my hand on it to keep it steady. The Me-109's circled overhead like hungry sharks. They worked their way around us by putting their backs to the sun before they were ready for the run.

Now the YO YO started in earnest. Six stayed up and six came down. We were trapped. We could not climb out of the valley. We had to stay where we were. Frantically, we tried to radio for help, but to no avail. We had VHF radios that were only good for a line-of-sight operation. We were so far below the top of the mountains that there was absolutely no possible way for our Squadron to hear us. I can't believe it. Just how did this happen? Where in hell is our Squadron top cover?

As the Me-109's worked their way behind us, we automatically tightened up in a right echelon formation. They came screaming down on us. Six came down and six stayed up. Looking back up and over my shoulder I can see the bright yellow noses, indicating that they were from the famed Herman Goering's Luftwaffe fleet. Red flames licking out from their guns were thirsting for the kill as they came at us with a real vengeance.

Black puffs of smoke broke out all around my ship. I was at this point, absolutely fascinated and watched in disbelief. It was all make-believe. Like little kids with little toy sparkler guns just spitting away at me. Only these were not toy guns.

I crunched behind my armour plate as the slugs kept exploding all around me. I kept praying, yet asking myself, "How can they miss?" . . . Just about this time I was snapped back to reality by a loud cry on the radio.

"*BREAK LEFT! DAMMIT, BREAK LEFT!*" We had such a tight formation, I feared that we would collide with one another.

Maintaining our tight formation, we made a lufberry maneuver towards the diving ships.

The first six zoomed on up and out of range. Round one and no hits. How can we be so lucky?

Down came the next six, and the same procedure was followed. Only this time we got a hit on one of the Me-109's. It was unfortunate we could not follow its path as we had several other ships to contend with. As a result, we were not able to claim a victory, even though we were sure we got one. We did not see the plane crash or the pilot bail out.

This was the least of our worries, as the next gang lined up ready to give us another YO YO. Our minds were really beginning to click now, and we were able to at least talk on the radio, and react accordingly.

I thought, "*Lord, is this ever going to end?*" "*We can't be this lucky forever.*" It seemed that we were in this dog-fight all afternoon. They had so many runs against us, I actually lost track.

FINALLY . . . they were gone . . . but were they really? Was this one of their traps?

We had to get up out of this valley and soon. We were getting low on fuel. Could it be possible that they too were low on fuel and left for this same reason?

Finally the decision was made. "*LET'S ALL GET THE HELL OUT OF HERE!*" came this voice on the radio.

I questioned, "But what if this is a trap?"

"I'm real low on gas," shot back another voice.

"It looks like we have no choice," I replied.

With that, we climbed on up and over the top of the mountains and everyone had vanished, both ours and theirs. This nagged all of us to the point where it was a tough decision to try and leave. But just where in hell was our Squadron that was supposed to act as our protective cover?

We were four visibly shaken kids, now apparently safe and on our way home. Yes, there is no doubt about it . . . Our Squadron was definitely gone, and so were the Me-109's.

Upon our arrival back at our base, we found our top cover of twelve ships had gotten home a short time before we did. We were advised that they were doing their job of protection all right, (over the wrong valley) while we were getting, *ONE BIG YO . . . YO . . .*

Young German pilots preparing the ME109 for battle. This type of aircraft was similar to the 12 used in Chapter 8, "*The Yo-Yo.*"
(Photo courtesy U.S. Air Force Museum.)

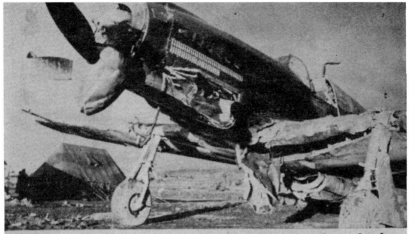

Looking like some weird insect whose neck has been broken, this battle-damaged P-51, veteran of 63 missions, was landed by its pilot at an airfield in the Mediterranean theater.

Captain Froome's ship after the mission in the chapter *"Most of Both."*
(Photo courtesy Savage collection.)

Chapter 9
Most of Both

L ooking around at our Squadron pilots, it was quite evident we were all very young. I qualified as one of the youngest at a ripe old age of 20 going on 21. Our CO was the old man at 40.

This day started off normal enough as our Squadron formed up and proceeded out over the Salerno Bay area towards the front. Suddenly one of our guys spots a lone Me-109 below. Breaking away he goes down and gets on its tail and surprises the German pilot completely. Concentrating on his victim, he puts another burst into the ship. It's a useless gesture now as the Me-109 is completely enveloped in flames and the pilot bails out. Fascinated by this event our man fails to realize that an Me-109 is now on his tail.

Our Squadron leader sees this and yells, "Caparelli, go down and protect him."

Obeying the order, Joe dives down and gets on this Me-109's tail. Out of nowhere comes another Me-109 on Joe's tail. It is now a free for all. The rest of the Squadron takes up the pursuit.

Incredible! It's hard to know who is doing what. Parachutes appear like popcorn all over the sky. Burning ships, ours and theirs, go spinning, climbing and diving, everywhere.

A voice screams over the air, *"I'm hit!. . . I'm hit!. . . get a fix! get a fix!"* then silence.

Another voice breaks through. *"Someone get that bastard off my tail, I'm getting my ass shot off."*

"May Day! . . . May Day!" screams another. The radio airways are filled with all kinds of desperate messages. All of this was meshed in between the jubilant cries of *"I got him! . . . I got him!"*

And then it was all over as quickly as it started. The only visible survivor of the melee was a lone Me-109 limping for home.

Joe Caparelli got a victory but he also was one that bailed out. Drifting down he had a ringside seat for the whole show. It seemed all so unreal now that it's over. Looking down, he saw with horror that the wind was carrying him into the enemy lines. Slowly, ever so slowly, he edged closer and closer towards the German lines, but it was no use.

About 300 or so feet above the ground, he watched in disbelief as a German soldier on the ground calmly raised his rifle and started shooting at him. Less than 200 feet now, he felt a sharp hot pain hit his upper left leg. Then he knew he had been shot as another slug tore through his lower left leg. Hanging helpless in his chute, he could only wait for the final blow.

Fortunately, he was blown further away from this soldier's shooting range. Now he hit the ground with a sickening thud. Before long, he was surrounded by Germans and made prisoner. Taken to a German field hospital, a doctor worked on his wounds. He set his smashed leg and then he was shipped out to a prison camp. It wasn't until about two weeks later as he began to get up and around that he noticed his usual 5'10" was now 5'8". The doctor had set his left leg two inches short. Well, at least he was alive.

On another mission, five ships were assigned to attack and destroy a group of dug-in German Tiger tanks. Don Wenger was the number three man in the dive. As he got in firing position, the German tank with its 88's zeroed in on him.

Taking a hit head-on, Don's ship became a huge torch as he pulled up into a vertical climb. At the top of his climb, the ship exploded into a big ball of flames. "My God, what a hell of a way to go," said the Colonel. It was a sad day for me as Don and I had been through a lot together.

About three months later, we got word through the grape vine that was impossible to believe. Don's alive and in prison camp! "But how can this be?" I ask, "three guys saw him get killed."

After the war, I got the whole story from Don. He bailed out at the top of the climb just as his ship exploded. He was severely burned all over his hands and face. Landing inside German lines, he was fortunate enough to get a German doctor that really cared. He received a lot of special medical care and experimental work on what was then called skin graft . . . now known as plastic surgery. Don showed me all the quilt marks on his butt. Incredibly, his face was like new. No way would any one ever know, except Don, just how much suffering and medical work that he had to go through.

On still another big dog-fight over Naples, "Shorty" Forbes went down in the bay. Safe and sound in his little dinghy raft, he waved to his buddies as they circled overhead.

Marking his location, and notifying Air Sea Rescue, everyone left feeling that "Shorty" would be back at the base in a couple of hours.

The RAF "Walrus" amphib went out to pick up Forbes. Circling around and around they were unable to find him in the raft. The wave swells were high enough to constantly block their view. So that day their valiant efforts failed. Night was falling and they had to give up until tomorrow.

The next day they were out at dawn criss-crossing the area, still searching and looking. Again failure. No one was particularly worried, after all didn't they get a good fix on him and send it to the RAF?

Actually Forbes was only about 10 miles or so off shore, so no one in the Squadron got overly excited. Why, if worst came to worst, he might even be able to paddle to shore. Day three came and went with the same results. Now it was official. Search and rescue was called off and Forbes was declared missing in action and presumed dead.

Shorty had seen them go over his dingy at least a dozen times. He waves confidently each time knowing that rescue was only minutes away. How wrong he was. After the third day, he realized that they were no longer looking for him. It was hard to understand that here he was so close to being rescued and now nothing.

He tried paddling with his hands, but the winds kept drifting him farther away from the land. The beachhead area was constantly in sight and now on the fourth day he thought it was now or never. He would swim the couple of miles to the beach. He slipped over the side in preparation for the swim, but in his weakened condition and with no food or water he thought better of it. He struggled back into the dinghy and fell back almost totally exhausted. He felt that he had better do something soon, as he was growing weaker by the hour.

Now driven almost insane by thirst, he tries to drink his own piss. *Ugh!* . . . it's not only salty but horrible as he retches in almost total convulsion.

Five days now and getting delirious he slips overboard in an attempt to end it all. The will to live is stronger than the desire to die. In a desperate effort, he is just barely able to climb back on board the rubber life raft.

The sun has been unmerciful. Burned, blistered beyond recognition, he lapses into unconsciousness.

On the sixth day, a guard patrolling the beach spots this yellow dingy on the shore. Going up to this raft, he is horrified to find Forbes.

More dead than alive, he's rushed to the hospital. Fortunately he just barely managed to survive this ordeal.

On another mission, a train was spotted rolling down the tracks and putting out a lot of smoke.

It only meant that he was really high-balling it to get to the station. Twelve of our ships dove down to finish off this train. It didn't take long as they lined up and methodically started to hit all the cars including the engine.

Fromme's ship was lined up on the box cars immediately behind the steam engine. The rest of the ships were in trail and spaced all along the train in preparing to finish off the luckless victim. Diving down, guns blazing, the whole train seems to explode at once in a big fireball. As he hit this ammo box car all types of junk went flying in the air. Fromme, now committed, has no choice but to fly through it. Before he gets in the clear, his ship is hit by several parts of the train.

Coming out of the holocaust, his first clear view was a huge tree directly in front of him. Unable to dodge it, he hits it head on. Staggering back up in the air, he limps for home. Parts of the train and tree are embedded in his ship. Now with the job done, he desperately fights for control of his ship.

Clawing his way up and out of the blazing freight train inferno below, he calls, "Red Leader One, I'm badly damaged and I'm not sure I can make it back."

"Stand by, and we will fly over to you and take a look," comes the reply from Red One.

Now within ten feet of Fromme, Red One looks with disbelief, and gasps silently. "Are you sure you can still keep your ship airborne?" he asks Fromme.

"No, I'm not sure. The engine is running very rough and the oil temperature is almost off the peg, controls are acting strange, but I'm still running," says Fromme.

"Roger, I'll stay with you as we head for home," he says.

Looking over the crippled ship, he just can't imagine how Fromme is still alive, much less fly this wreck back to the base.

The canopy's still intact, but the rest of the ship's condition is beyond description. It looks like he had crashed already. The leading edges of the wing look like they have been worked over by a large giant's hand. It hardly resembles a wing at all. Smashed, bent, squeezed. But that's not all.

Red One moves in a little closer and stares in disbelief at the nose section. It has huge dents and lodged in the nose between the nose guns, *is a tree limb about the size of a man's arm.*

"That's impossible, a tree limb couldn't possibly get through the whirling three bladed prop and between the guns," he said to his flight, "but it's there just the same."

"It's incredible, that's all, incredible," said Red Two. Still looking over Fromme's ship in utter disbelief, he can see parts of . . . *Holy cow! Naw it just can't be, but it is.*

It looks like actual parts of a whistle from that train.

"Hang in there Fromme," came Red One's voice. Due to the slow flight speed, the rest of the Squadron had to circle to keep up. Each in turn flies in for a close look and all are in complete disbelief that he even stands a ghost of a chance of making it. It's a miracle he is still flying, much less being able to get back home.

He did make it back and landed unhurt: His ship was a total wreck. He won the DFC (Distinguished Flying Cross) for his flying and surviving this mission.

Two weeks later he was shot down and killed.

On another mission, Lt. Price another pilot in our Squadron was shot down and never heard from again. It was noted that he was first MIA (Missing In Action) than KIA (Killed In Action). It wasn't until a year later that he turns up back in our Squadron. No one recognized him. He had put on considerable weight. Going from 130 pounds to almost 250 pounds.

I saw him a short time later and asked, "What in the hell happened to you, Price? We all thought you were dead."

"When I got shot down," said Price, "an Italian farmer found me before the Germans did. He took me in and hid me in his dirt potato cellar. I ate and ate and no exercise did a lot to help me gain all this weight.

After a couple of weeks he felt sorry for me. So he sent his daughter down to keep me company. I was in no hurry to be liberated. Believe me, it was a tough life. Almost a year of living hell."

There was no question about our Squadron having the, Most of Both.

Our Squadron, the 16th later called the 522, had the most number of confirmed victories in the 27th Group. But in turn, it also had the most number of losses.

The RAF "Walrus" similar to the types that were used to search and rescue downed flyers in the Med.
(Photo courtesy U.S. Air Force Museum.)

Chapter 10
A Major Decision

A fter almost a year in combat and 30 missions, I was given the option of going on leave. "Why do I need to do this?" I asked the Flight Surgeon.

"It's to help you guys get a rest and a break from all the tension," he said. "This is an experimental two week rest program that we plan to initiate, starting out with you and a few of your friends."

"I really don't need or want to," I replied, "I'm anxious to finish my tour and go home."

"I understand," he said, "but this is a new policy that we now have started and feel that you have had your share of missions and mishaps and deserve this break."

At this time no one had any idea about combat fatigue. When I first came overseas, 10 missions was considered as a full tour. Then it soon became 15, 25, 100 and now the number of missions for a tour was unlimited.

Still fighting this new program, I reluctantly agreed to take one week's leave on the Isle of Capri. The doctor said, "Take one week, see how you feel and maybe as an option you might want to take an additional week."

"No way, Sir, I'm not about to abandon my buddies."

"You're not doing that," he said, "it's just a break in your tour."

I packed my bag and gave my, "I'll be back in a week or less," comment to all of my comrades as I made preparations for this leave.

The Isle of Capri is located in the Mediterranean Sea, west of Naples, Italy. It had been the playground of Roman Emperors. As we approached the docks, I looked up in awe at the huge cliffs with all the stone houses that had been built into the small crags in the rocks.

I soon found out that I'm not the only American pilot assigned to this rest camp. About a dozen of us were selectively chosen to participate in this experimental program. Checking in to the hotel, I was absolutely sure that I would be back with my outfit before the end of the week. A bell boy met me at the door and after checking in, he escorted me up to my room.

Unbelievable . . . a big clean soft bed . . . *white sheets* . . . I haven't seen this in almost a year, white bath and face towels, etc. all the comforts of home.

During supper I met a pilot by the name of Walsh. He was from one of the other Squadrons of our Group. We became real good friends and shared all of our experiences. Comparing notes, it was evident that my Squadron was by far the best of the three.

We both tried to put all this behind us now as we lapped up the fine luxuriousness of this hotel. Just think, we had personal maid service for whatever our need. I hadn't slept in a bed or had white sheets in over a year.

Unfortunately, the people here were still very much pro-German. We were treated like second class citizens, and they (Italians) made it quite clear that the Luftwaffe were far superior to the U.S. pilots. Could be it was the classy uniforms of the Luftwaffe that helped do it. At any rate, the feeling was there and we were reminded of it on more than one occasion.

The third night we witnessed a tremendous artillery fire fight about fifty miles or so north of Naples. It lasted all night and it made both of us think how lucky we were to be here and away from the fight.

The next day we decided to take a row boat trip to the Blue Grotto Cave located on the Island. Waiting for the right time and wave swell, our boatman paddled furiously for the small opening that would let us gain entrance to the huge cave.

Adjusting our eyes to the dim light, we were completely awe struck and it took our breath away as we gazed at all of the magnificent colors that suddenly popped into our view. We spent an hour in the cave and then made an exit just as spectacular as our entrance.

Touring the area, we saw all kinds of artists works in cameo and shells. We were real sucker tourists for this stuff and the natives knew it. War? What war? These people were so remotely removed from the real brutal harshness of war it was almost to the point where they had absolutely no feeling as to what was going on.

Later that night during dinner, we had a beautiful serenade by the local musicians.

A violin and accordion made for a pretty good combination. Unfortunately, a lot of the men over there think they're as great as Caruso, and we had to suffer silently through this.

Perhaps they felt that this would get more money from us. Yes we did give them more, but it was for them to leave rather than stay.

During the later part of that week at dinner, Walsh asked me the usual questions about my home and family. Exchanging basic facts, it soon became apparent that he had started putting some very intelligent questions and thoughts into my mind.

"Do you mean to tell me that you have 30 missions and you still can't go home?"

"That's right," I replied, "it's up to the Flight Surgeon when one can leave."

"What's the deal with your family?" he continued, "Didn't you say that you are the sole support of your Mom and eight kids, since your Dad got killed?"

"That's right," I replied and now I know he has touched on points for me to seriously ponder.

Walsh then says, "Didn't you tell me about having two real bad crashes this past two weeks?"

"You're right again, I guess you were listening to me after all," I said.

"Well Doc, I think you should consider getting the hell out of combat right now." This conversation was getting nowhere fast, so Walsh dropped it.

The next day he said, "Why don't you ask for another week before you decide.

"Decide what?" I asked, but got no answer.

"Well, why not?" I said, as I sent word back to the Squadron requesting the one week extension. The next week went by faster than the first and

I knew that the seed had been planted and was now in the germinating stage.

Arriving back with my outfit, I was welcomed with open arms. Everyone wanted to know more about the fabulous rest camp called the Isle of Capri.

Back on combat duty, I was on an armed recon flight with twelve other ships, and we ready for anything. We had seen nothing for over an hour and about all the shooting we did was at the insulators on the high tension power lines. Turning left up the valley, two of us spotted a motorcycle with a side car and dispatch rider winding his way up the mountainous trail. I know that this sounds like a familiar tale but this really happened. Surprise is the key. As we got close enough to fire a few rounds we were way off target. The tracers hit behind and ricochetted out in front of them.

Looking back quite startled, the rider then gave his cycle full power. Another burst from the guns, Damn, too far this time. Constantly looking back, attention diverted, he had overlooked the fact that they were on this mountain type of road. They rapidly approached this big curve and the last view we had of them was their fantastic take-off out over the valley.

Approaching Lake Como, I saw about a half dozen fishing boats, with the crews waving at us. Then, *OH NO!* one of our guys decides to powder them. We're all aghast at this.

"*Stop! stop!*" comes a voice over the radio, but too late. We all felt terrible except this joker. Arriving back at the base, we could only say one thing to this jerk.

"*Boy, you really are a tiger,* that's it, *TIGER, SCOURGE OF THE LUFTWAFFE.*" A name that stuck with him for as long as he was with us.

On another particular mission, we surprised a convoy of trucks bound for Rome. We counted almost thirty in this bunch. It was a picture perfect mission. We came over the hill and there they were, on the roll. A large cloud of dust marking their trail.

On the first pass they never knew what hit them. About a third of them were left burning as we pulled up for the next pass. I came screaming down on this pass and hit three trucks. I watched in awe as the men seemed to just jump up about 15 to 20 feet in the air. I looked again and realized that, *good God! these guys weren't jumping. It was my 50 calibre bullets that caused this.*

Pulling up over-head, I decided that I had enough of this carnage. I watched the angels of death deal out their message and felt half-sick. It wasn't too long and it was over as fast as it started. A huge pall of smoke now hung over the valley as we started for home.

This particular day was a gloomy one. We all welcomed this break from our daily routine of combat.

Brodie and I were relaxing in our tent playing cards when we hear this loud roar of a twin-engine airplane overhead.

"Hey, Brodie!" I say, "I can't believe any fool would be flying on a day like this."

"Neither can I, Doc," replied Brodie, as we both got up and left our tent to try and see who was nuts enough to be flying around in this crud.

It looks like a lot of other guys must have had the same idea as we glance around at the large group that had gathered outside of the tent area all looking up at the cloudy rainy sky. Suddenly we see a ship break out of the clouds.

"I'll be damned, it's a German Me-110!" I yell to Brodie.

He rapidly disappears back up in the clouds as our air raid sirens kicked off their belligerent howl.

"Probably got lost," remarks Brodie.

About ten minutes later we hear him again and it sounds like he's coming back. Just about this same time we hear a loud scream and then, *Bam!* a loud bomb blast rocks our area. Everyone ducks for cover. It was over as quickly as it began.

We both see this guy staggering up towards us. He looked like he just climbed out of a mud bath.

"Whoo eee! you stink like a skunk," says Brodie. "What in hell happened to you?"

"When the bomb fell, I looked for the closest hole I could find," exclaimed Bob, "and that just happened to be the mess hall's grease pit."

All of his clothes had to be buried and it took several hours in the hot shower before anyone dared to get near him.

After my 35th mission, I got an appointment with the CO to advise him of my decision. Reporting to the Colonel, I said, "Colonel, Sir, I really need to get out of combat."

"*You what? . . . Why?* . . . don't you realize we have you scheduled for one of the Squadron's key leaders?" he said.

"No, Sir," I said, "but, I think that after you hear my story, you will agree with me."

I remember about our Capri conversation and yes indeed, Walsh was right.

The Colonel did not want to lose me, but after listening to my story, reluctantly agreed to arrange for me to fly over to the Flight Evaluation Board in Foggia, Italy.

Chapter 11
The Verdict

The 27th Fighter Bomber Group had a UC-78 available for executive transport. This ship was a small fabric covered twin-engine Cessna. It was built for the Air Force, but was more commonly known as the "Twin Breasted Cub." It wasn't much of an airplane, but it did serve its purpose. I didn't feel like I was a special VIP but I did get assigned a trip in this ship when the time came for my meeting in Foggia with the Flight Evaluation Board.

Bob Barnett, a friend of mine, would be the pilot. Climbing aboard with my chute, he said, "Doc, you really lucked out."

"How's that?" I said.

"Well, you just might get assigned to a post back in the states, and that would be great, replied Bob.

"Dream on, dream on," I replied, secretly hoping that he just might be right.

After an uneventful flight from Salerno to Foggia, we touched down at the Foggia airport. Foggia was the home of the evaluation Board headquarters.

I was visibly nervous waiting for my turn with the Board. Despite the fact that I felt very confident about my case. Several other guys had gone before me and received very rough treatment.

Entering the hearing room, I was met with some very heavy brass.

There was nothing less than a Major's rank present. Introducing myself to all the Board members, I proceeded to tell them in full detail the reasons why I felt my combat duty should be terminated.

They were patient and understanding and listened to everything I had to say. It took about thirty minutes or so to cover all the details. I was then given the opportunity for a question and answer period.

One Colonel said, "Do you really mean you are the sole support of your Mother and eight kids in New York?"

"Yes, Sir," I replied.

"Is it also true that you have had two very serious fighter aircraft type crashes in two weeks?" asks another.

"Yes, Sir," I reply again.

"Please tell the Board all about them," says the chairman, a full bird Colonel. I proceeded to give them the full story about the failed engines, the unique airport with the gear up crash-landing in the ammo dump, and the crash landing into the side of a hill.

They listened with politeness and then started talking with each other. "OK, Lieutenant. You may leave now. Wait outside and we will advise you of our decision," said the Colonel.

In less than a half hour, I was summoned back into the Board hearing room. "We all have reviewed your combat record, missions, awards and mishaps," said the Colonel continuing, "and it is the finding of this board that you are to be assigned a unit of your choice, non-combat of course."

I can hardly believe me ears. "Now," continued the Colonel, "in honor of your service we would like to offer you a choice."

"What the hell are they talking about?" I thought. "Everytime I had a choice I usually got the bad end of a deal."

"You may pick one of three options," he continues. "The Training Command, Transport Command, or the Ferry Command."

Not being aware of what was to come, I thought for a minute and decided silently, why not the Ferry Command? This would put me back in the States and I would be ferrying new ships from the west coast to the east coast and visa-versa.

If I chose the Training Command, I would probably wind up teaching flying and I felt that I really wasn't ready for that type of flying. Transport? No way, they were slow and I really enjoyed flying the fighters too much to get myself snookered into that one.

"OK, my mind's made up," I said to the Colonel. "Sir, it looks like I would like the Ferry Command."

Cessna UC-78. Better known as the "Bamboo Bomber." A similar one like this was used in "The Verdict". (Photo courtesy U.S. Air Force Museum.)

"Fine, good choice, son. Good Luck." The Colonel rose and shook my hand and said, "Your orders will be cut shortly."

Boy, that was quick, I thought, as I went outside to await my orders that would send me home to the States.

It seemed forever before a sergeant came down the hall with my papers. I was really excited now as the sergeant, handing me the orders, said, "Good luck, Sir."

I could hardly wait to go out and tell Bob the good news. He had been waiting outside not knowing what to expect. I rushed up to him and said, "Guess what? I got my orders to the Ferry Command," waving the papers in front of his face.

"Great," he said, "when do you have to report and what is the name of the new station in the United States?"

"You know, Bob, I was so excited I really didn't take the time to look," I replied. "Boy, I can't wait to get back to the States and civilization again," I sang out. "Just think, cold milk, ice cream, American girls. It is almost too good to be true."

After all our jubilation, I thought now would be the time to share my good fortune and new state side location with Bob.

Opening up the envelope with the orders, I started to read aloud. "Lt. Mark A. Savage . . . the Flight Evaluation Board after due deliberation has found all of the facts to be true. In consideration of your past efforts, you are hereby given your first choice of assignment, *The Overseas Ferry Command*."

"*What! . . . What does this mean?*" I moaned. Bob grabbed my orders and continued, "You are to report to Maison Blanche, North Africa, no later than 10 days from the date of these orders.

"Well, you lucked out all right," Bob said, "but not what you had originally thought."

As the shock slowly wore off, I pulled myself back from my dreams to reality and asked Bob, "Just what do you think this really means for me?"

"All you can do is wait and see," he says.

It was late afternoon when we climbed aboard the UC-7 for our flight back home to the Salerno base. The weather was fine for visual flight and now, I'm on my way with orders to report to the Ferry Command.

We were all in a rather relaxed mood as we flew along at 8,500 feet elevation just over the top of the mountains. Looking out over this terrain gives one a reason to enjoy the flight that much more, knowing that you do not have to drive those crooked roads that wind all through and around the mountains.

Then without warning, the left engine starts backfiring and missing. Our hearts missed a lot of beats too. Bob's hands were all over the controls. Mixtures, props, throttles, gas selectors, but nothing really helped at this time.

I put my chute on and made ready to bail out. This dumb twin had no way to feather a prop.

Now with the left engine wind-milling the whole ship began vibrating badly. This in turn put such a negative drag on the good engine that we were unable to hold altitude. We were going down to a sure crash.

"Hey, Bob, what is our altitude now?" I yell.

"*We're down to 7,000 feet,*" he says, "*and sinking fast. I can't hold it and it looks bad.*"

"*Damn, it's time to leave this hunk of shit,*" I yell.

"*You can't now,*" Bob said excitedly, "*we're too low! . . . we're too low!*

"What do you mean, we're at 7,000 feet," I said.

"You're right, Doc, but did you look out? The ground is less than 500 feet away. You'll never get the chute open in time."

Before I got a chance to say anything else we lose another 400 feet. Now we are close to the ground and it looks for sure that we will soon be on it, whether we like it or not.

Suddenly a small pass appears in the mountains directly in front of us. "That will lead us down into the Salerno Valley," says Bob, "*I hope!*"

At this point in the game, I am willing to try anything. Seizing this golden opportunity, Bob banks the ship and makes for the small pass in the mountains. God, I sure hope that we can make it.

We barely skim through this pass with just inches to spare. Both of us can now start breathing a little easier as the ground rapidly falls away and we appear to gain altitude automatically.

We are now down to 3,000 feet and still sinking, but at least we are keeping pace and do not appear to be fighting a losing battle.

Around 2,000 feet the engine suddenly clears up and starts running smoothly again. "Boy, that's strange," says Bob.

I tell Bob, "Well, at least, when you fly the single engine fighters, you know for sure whether it will fly, one way or the other. You never get suckered into a stupid situation like this."

"Right on, Doc," says Bob, as he drops the gear and banks the ship in for a landing at the home base of the 27th Fighter/Bomber Group on the Salerno beachhead airport.

**Foggia, Italy was the home base of many groups of B-17's as pictured here.
(Photo courtesy of U.S. Air Force Museum.)**

Flight of 2 A-24's — 1942.
(Photo courtesy of U.S. Air Force Museum.)

A row of P-47's ready for action.
(Photo courtesy U.S. Air Force Museum.)

Flight of three ME 110's.
(Photo courtesy U.S. Air Force Museum.)

Savage pictured with the P-47, "Thunderbolt".
(Photo courtesy Savage collection.)

B-26, Marauder over the coast of Italy, 1943.
(Photo courtesy Army Air Corps.)

15th Air Force, bomb strikes and bombs away, oil targets, Vienna, Austria.
(Photo courtesy Military Allied Air Force.)

The P-51 could not sustain flak damage like the P-47.

Fragmentation effect on the elevator of a P-47.

8 mm railway attery of four ak guns.

Damaged vertical stabilizer of a P-47.

50 caliber bullets striking an FW-190.

German airfield JU-88's destroyed by low level attacks.

Example of
bridge busting.

B-17 crash-
landed in
Switzerland.

Luftwaffe units
based in Italy.

Damaged tail
section of a
'Thunderbolt' P-47.

German 88 mm
and 105 mm
coastal guns.

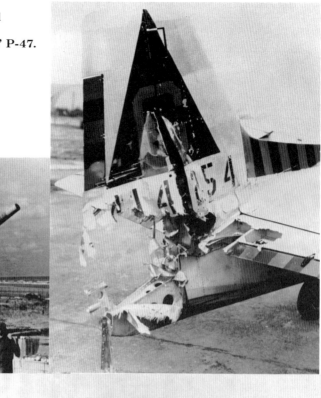

Typical German
20 mm anti-
aircraft guns.

Left wing
damage
to a P-47.

Chapter 12
The Multi-Engine Rating

I had been reassigned from combat to this overseas Ferry Command, and in a way I was looking forward to the new assignment as I checked into the headquarters at Maison Blanche at Algiers, North Africa. Actual assignment date was still several days off, so I thought it would be an excellent time to visit the city of Algiers. It had been settled by the French and I felt in some ways was one of the better places I had seen in North Africa.

That night, I was in the Officer's club bar drinking with my new found friends of the Ferry Squadron, when about 11:20 PM the air raid sirens started wailing their tune. "That's probably just a drill," I was assured by Chuck Leedham, as most of us were not feeling too much pain by now.

In about ten minutes we started to hear the distant bom-bom of the anti-aircraft guns. Since we were in such a good mood (well oiled) we all decided to go out with drinks in hand to watch the show. The searchlights were playing all over the sky looking for the enemy bombers. It wasn't too long before the ships were overhead and the bombs were beginning to fall. Incredible! Why would they come way down here to bomb us? Could it be because of our large supply of new aircraft now stored here? At any rate, I had dropped a lot of bombs and now it was my turn to be on the receiving end. Even though I was pretty drunk, I felt real fear as the bombs came closer.

Dropping our drinks, we all dove for the nearest shelter we could find, an open water ditch. This helped sober us up in a hell of a hurry. It made us all much older and wiser as we made our way back to the BOQ (Bachelor's Officers Quarters).

A few days later I was called in by our CO, a Colonel, who asked me, "Son, are you Multi-Engine rated?"

"No Sir, I am not," I replied. "I just got out of a Mustang Fighter Squadron."

"Well, you had better get rated, because tomorrow you are scheduled to ferry one. I suggest that you get with an officer named Lt. Leedham for a check flight," he said.

"Yes Sir," I replied.

I met Chuck Leedham on the flight line and he told me, "You're to read this book tonight, because tomorrow you will be flying this particular ship when you complete the blindfold test.

Actually you will be blindfolded, and you must be able to show me the position of all the instruments and controls on the ship. After that," he said, "I'll check you out."

"OK, but what kind of a ship are you talking about?" I asked.

"Why, it's a P-38," he said.

My only response was, "*WOW! . . . REALLY?*"

Now I must admit, I was a bit nervous as we did a walk around for the preflight of the P-38, and completed the required blindfold tests.

"OK, let's get on with it," said Chuck.

"I'll be ready," I assured him.

"Fine, Doc," said Chuck, "But," he cautioned me, "be sure you understand the correct use of the crossfeed valves."

Again going over the procedures for starting, emergency gear, he left me with this final warning. "Be sure and run up your engines with high enough power to get your superchargers to cut in prior to letting off on the brakes. Use 10 degrees of flaps on take off if you like."

Finally he then said, "OK, are you ready to go? Any final questions?"

I couldn't think of anything he didn't cover, so I answered him by shaking my head no, and saying "Roger," as I tightened up my seat belt and shoulder harness. Starting up the Allison engines, I called for taxi and take-off clearance. As I taxied out, I really enjoyed listening to the smooth melodic sound of the two engines. It was like running a twin engine Chris Craft motor boat.

I tried to remember all of the myriad of instructions by Chuck, as I checked everything out, being particularly careful about the fuel selectors.

Calling the Tower I request take-off clearance for a closed pattern flight with several touch-and-go's with the option for full stop landings.

Chuck said, "If you can do three successful take offs and landings, we can officially check you out and sign off your log book with a multi-Engine rating."

As I push the throttles full forward, holding the brakes, I waited for the turbochargers to cut in. I can still hear Chuck saying, "Remember, they both have to cut in and stabilize before you let go of the brakes."

I feel the ship jump as I let go of the brakes. The P-38 accelerates and I immediately pull back on the wheel. The ship leaps into the air and goes straight up in a vertical climb.

Chuck almost faints as I continue going straight up.

This is great, no torque. I could never do this with the Mustang. I finally realize that this is not the normal way to take off as I started to push the nose forward to assume a more normal type of climb.

Leveling off at 2,000 feet, I finally start to breathe easier again as I try to get the feel of this machine. After that initial take off, everything else is anti-climatic.

I shot three landings and take-offs and then took it out of the area to get the feel of the ship. Far enough away from the local airport, I did a few rolls, loops, and stalls to try and get the full feeling of this most magnificent fighter ship. No doubt about it, I am in love. I still, down deep, prefer the P-51, but this ship sure runs a close second.

Calling in to the Tower, I reluctantly start back to the field. I feel now that I really understand this ship, despite the fact I have had only a little over an hour in it.

After my last landing, I taxied back to the parking area where Chuck is waiting for me. I was pleased at the way this ship handled and how comfortable I felt in it. Much more so than my original first flight in the P-51. I am looking forward to flying the P-38 cross-country in the next few days.

Cutting the engines, Chuck was right there to greet me and explain. "God, Doc, you gave me one hell of a fright on that first take off. Well, everything is OK now," he says as he signs my log book to show, yes, it's official.

I am now a legally rated Multi-Engine pilot.

The Lockheed "Lightning" similar to the type used in the Multi-Engine rating. (Photo courtesy U.S. Air Force Museum.)

The Boston Havoc, A-20 Light Attack Bomber.
(Photo courtesy U.S. Air Force Museum.)

Chapter 13
Fire In The Hole

As a Ferry Pilot we generally faced a lot of unique problems. One in particular was how to get back after the delivery. At this time we had been picking up the brand new fighters and flying them from Casablanca to Oran, Algiers and Tunis. Their limited range forced us to stop at these places for fuel.

Over the past few months, we were able to keep up with the Depot assembly program as long as they were shipped over via the "Liberty" transport ships. This all changed dramatically when a Navy aircraft carrier brought in a load of airplanes. The carrier had the capacity to bring in the new ships to the point that we could hardly keep up with the delivery program. They usually off-loaded almost three times as many airplanes than any other transport. Of course, this was not the usual means to bring them over, as they (carriers) were urgently needed in the Pacific combat area.

We had been informed that a carrier was due in soon, so the word was out to get as many airplanes ferried to Tunis before the next big load was dumped on us. A flight of eight P-51's made their way across North Africa and arrived safely at Tunis, North Africa, the last jumping off place prior to the combat area. Pick-up was scheduled for early afternoon with a return to Casablanca late in the evening.

Our pick-up ship was an old converted Boston Havoc A-20. A fast noisy twin. A bit limited for passenger space, but that didn't matter as the trip was never that long. This was a particular special A-20. It had all of the interior removed and could squeeze five people in its bomb bay area. Yes, it was cramped, but it was a lot better than staying overnight. Generally the flight was just a bit under two hours. The A-20 had a fair range and did not have to stop for fuel.

I was extremely disappointed when it was announced that there would not be enough room to take all of us back. This meant that we would have to stay overnight in the BOQ (Bachelors Officers Quarters), not too appealing since it was only temporary and quite sparse. The next shuttle was not due in till late the next day.

Our lucky buddies bade us good bye as they climbed into the belly of the Havoc. Communications was established via an extension line from the pilot's compartment back to the bomb bay. Seats were almost nil and due to extreme noise, conversation was held to the minimum. The pilot fired up the ship and took off west bound for the home base of Casablanca.

Just about the time he leveled off at 6,000 feet, everyone in the bomb-bay noticed a strong smell of gasoline fumes. They tried to contact the pilot, but to no avail . . . all of their communications were dead.

No smoking for sure now, as they tried to figure out how to tell the pilot of this peril. Putting on their chutes, they felt that maybe with luck perhaps they just might get an opportunity to bail out if he slowed it down just a little bit. But now at cruise speed, it would be impossible to bail out.

After a short shouting conference, it was felt that maybe when he slowed down for the landing and dropped the gear, they would all attempt to get out at that time, via their chutes.

The pilot of the A-20 set up and began a full and complete tactical approach to the Casablanca Airport. It might be he wanted to impress the ex-fighter jocks inside his ship. So far, so good.

But the strong smell of fumes was getting worse. Due to the high speed approach and low altitude, they would have to stay with the ship and hope for the best.

At the top of his climb, the pilot dropped gear and flaps and fortunately kept the power on. The A-20 had a strange characteristic habit of constant popping and backfiring when power was reduced to idle in a glide. Everyone inside the bomb bay knew this, and could only hope it would not create a hazard with all the gasoline vapors floating around inside the bomb bay.

The A-20 "Boston Havoc." Quite similar to the one in the story about, *"Fire in the Hole"*. (Photo courtesy of U.S. Air Force Museum.)

Everyone had kept their chutes on during the entire flight, hoping that they might have the opportunity to bail out.

As the ship made its downwind leg and base leg turn, the pilot did keep up the power. Now base to final . . . same thing . . . so far so good.

Just about at the point of touch down, the throttles were pulled off and both engines barked out their familiar popping sounds.

It only took a second or two before the exploding exhaust flames found the fume-filled bomb-bay compartments.

A large ball of flame engulfed the five guys as they made a hasty exit out of the bomb bay compartment via the bottom trap door. First one, two, then the rest came tumbling out each one in turn hitting the gravel runway with his chute, face and then head as they bumped down the gravel runway in pursuit of the A-20. Finally coming to a stop. Dazed . . . burnt, and bewildered.

Meanwhile the A-20 continued on down the runway. The pilot unaware of what was happening saw the Fire trucks rushing up to meet him as he turned off the runway and stopped. He was quite puzzled by all the fire trucks and ambulances moving in his direction.

His radio was out and he had absolutely no idea as to what was happening.

Opening up the hatch, he stared back in disbelief at his ship. Now in total shock, all he could see was the cockpit, wings and engines. Everything else had been consumed by fire. He had no idea as to what happened to his passengers. For all he knew they could be dead.

Shutting down his engines he made a hasty exit, afraid now that the gas tanks in the wings would blow. All the fire trucks could do was just stand by and watch the flames consume the rest of the ship.

The ambulances picked up the five very lucky guys and rushed them to the hospital for treatment of burns and embedded cinders.

Everyone survived, but it had been just pure luck with that type of, *Fire in the Hole . . .*

A C-47 (DC-3) also known in the RAF as the "Dakota." Similar to the one in the story, *"Capadichino Catastrophe"*.
(Photo courtesy U.S. Air Force Museum.)

Chapter 14
Capodichino Catastrophe
(Capo-da-chino)

It took a while for me to realize that flying the C-47 (DC-3) wasn't all bad. I must admit that the first time my orders came sending me on this detail to fly the C-47, I was mentally sick. The gear speed of the P-51 (150 mph) was the cruising speed of the C-47. I mumbled and grumbled and hated every day that I had to fly this lumbering slow truck.

Then one day everything dramatically changed. The schedule called for a pick-up at the Casablanca airport in North Africa with the flight then scheduled to proceed on to Cairo, Egypt. I had not been to Cairo and this sort of trip should help give me a little incentive to get through this trying period. I thought.

As I arrived at the Casablanca airport, we picked up the manifest and discovered to our delight we were to have 20 flight nurses on board. Indeed, this would be my turning point. As those pretty American nurses climbed on board, I found the time to go back and visit and become acquainted with some real live American girls.

Coffee and sandwiches and friendly conversation left me in a highly charged state. "Why, no way could I do this with a fighter," I told myself. I couldn't believe that I had fought this program for so long.

Now a complete convert, I looked forward to flying this lumbering C-47 with a different respect. The ability to see more countries, fly longer distances, fly actual instruments and be able to go even in the bad weather, all somehow made real sense.

Of course, meeting those girls had nothing to do with it.

We had daily trips to someplace new in almost every country in Europe. They included mail runs, delivery of the Stars and Stripes daily newspapers, and flying personnel in and out of our theater to various rest camps. This included the Canes, Riviera in Monaco, Lido Beach, Florence, Italy, England and the other R & R (Rest & Recreation) areas. We even did some air evacuation of the wounded down to the hospital ships located in the Bay of Naples.

There were other trips to Egypt, Yugoslavia, Greece, Turkey, Crete, Austria, Germany, and France. All over. We did fly hard, but we also got plenty of R & R tossed in.

We had a beautiful sailboat called the "Sally," that a guy by the name of Garrison had somehow promoted or commandered for our personal use. Many of us spent hours and hours of our off duty time out sailing this boat in the Med.

Occasionally we would get back early from our trips and enjoy a walk in the downtown areas of Naples. The hardest part was the first time in Naples trying to get used to the smell. After we were there for a few hours we just didn't seem to notice it.

The people who constantly hawked everything and anything for a fee never ceased to amaze me. No one ever bought anything for the first asking price, except of course the Americans. I believe that the Italians loved to bargain and felt bad when we just paid them the first price that they asked.

Walking to my apartment along the Via Roma, I was constantly approached by young kids always begging for the choc-a-lotta, cig-r-rettes, chewin' gum. And, of course,

"Hey, Americano, do you want a woman?"

I constantly said, "No! I don't want a woman."

But this woman clean," they would say.

Again I said, repeating more firmly than before, "*No! No! I don't want one!*"

This kid would then come back with, "*But this woman, she virgin!*"

Naturally, I would respond, "That's nice. But, how do you know this?"

"That easy man, she my mother."

The weather had been bad all night and as we got up and prepared for today's schedule, we felt that perhaps everyone would be getting a late start.

Winding up the long hill towards the airport, we came upon a horse pulling a wagon loaded with about 12 people. The driver had a large stick and was beating hell out of this poor emaciated looking horse. It was doing its best to try and pull the load up the hill, but you could see that it was fighting a losing battle.

It was cold with a light drizzle falling. Steam could be seen coming out from all over the horse. Feeling sorry for this poor animal, we stopped to try and give some aid. About this time the horse fell down and laid on its side. Shouts, cursing, more beatings did not help get the poor horse up on its feet.

There was no way we could help now, so we pulled away and left this sad scene.

Arriving at the base operations, a notice was posted on the board and it said, "Weather being so bad in several areas many flight operations are scrubbed for the day, but you are requested to stand by until afternoon in case the flight conditions should improve. After that you are free to leave the field."

With this change of plans, I thought I would go downtown to the Officers Club for a late lunch.

Three of us had gotten in the jeep and were ready to leave and as usual, we toured the flight line checking on our ships before we left the field. Hearing this C-47 preparing for take-off, we waited and watched as he rolled down the runway, tail up, lift off, everything normal.

No matter how many times we see one take-off and land we always watch with rapture. I guess we were in love with this flying. There is no other answer.

Watching this guy go overhead, we hear a loud explosion. Then stare in horror as it dives for the ground. It hits with one hell of a crash and comes to a full stop. Standing here flabbergasted, we see nothing happen. No fire trucks, no ambulances, nothing. Then . . . a big explosion and a fire breaks out in the engine compartment and fuselage, or cabin area.

"Shouldn't we go out there and try to help?" I suggested.

"No way," says Jacobsen. "There's enough trouble without us being part of it."

"Look! One guy is coming out of the rear door," says Leedham. "Now two, three, but where is the fourth?"

Peering through the dense smoke and flames, we are horrified to see the pilot still sitting there in his seat and not moving. Flames are creeping up towards him. "I don't really understand why those guys won't go back and get him out of there," pleads Dollard.

It soon became apparent that no one was going back to help this poor unfortunate individual. The fire trucks, crash trucks and ambulances finally arrive on the scene. Making our way back to operations, we are all stunned by this tragedy.

We're not too hungry now as the rescue squads arrived to put out the fire and remove the body from the ship. It was a sad and useless accident. Preliminary investigation proved that this indeed was a preventable accident.

Prior to take-off, the radio man had the very pistol out, loaded a star shell in the chamber then cocked the pistol. He replaced the loaded and cocked pistol back in the usual place in the ceiling. There was a hole cut in the ceiling that would enable a person to fire the gun and shoot a flare outside of the ship.

On take-off, the gun somehow had slipped out of this locked position, fell to the floor and the force of the fall caused it to fire.

As the gun fired, the flare, or star shell, went on up and hit the ship's glycol tank. This tank contained a highly explosive alcohol anti-icing fluid. The tank exploded and fire erupted. The ship hit the ground in a slight side motion and the left prop sheared off slicing through the pilot's compartment. The pilot was killed instantly.

We did not know this at the time of the crash and fire. So this explains why there was no possible way that anyone could have saved this individual's life.

It was late afternoon by the time we were ready to leave for our downtown apartment. We were all back in the jeep and a bit down as a result of this terrible accident.

Coming around the bend on that winding road back to the city of Naples, we spotted the place where that horse incident took place that morning. There was roughly about a dozen people sitting around a smouldering fire. I said to Chuck Leedham, "Isn't this the same place we saw that horse go down this morning?"

"It sure is," he replied.

We can see several people still eating and some picking their teeth. They are paying no attention to us as we stop and watch them. The fire is almost out now and the smoke hangs over the area in a pall like manner as if to signify this occasion.

Next to these people is the empty horse-drawn cart. Nearby are the back bones, rib cage, and skeleton remains of the horse. It's all that's left to indicate that this was a live horse just a few short hours ago.

These Italians are full now. Some can be seen nearby sleeping off the big meal.

"It's probably their first real meal in a long time," I say sadly, to my buddies in the jeep.

MATS 328th Ferry Squadron's B-25 "Quanto Costa"—"How Much?" at the Capodichino Airport, Naples, Italy.

Chapter 15
The Boondoggle

It was during the later part of 1944 when we got the word from Headquarters about a unique idea. It seems that some General in the States decided that it might be possible to spur the sales of War Bonds to the public if he could get those old battle weary P-40's back to the United States for public display. The war in China had helped the public accept these ships as everyone knows about the Flying Tigers.

All of the P-40's carried many battle scars and no doubt would help significantly in whipping up public interest in this noble effort. Lined up in five rows of ten each, the 40's made a sad picture on the far side of the Pomigliano airport, near Naples, Italy. We personally knew that they hadn't flown in over two years, and very little effort had been made to mothball them.

Since the major conflict was still flaring in France, there was absolutely no way the Navy would commit a carrier to the Mediterranean to this task. Plans were to have a carrier from the States rendezvous at Casablanca within the next three weeks. This particular date was picked as Headquarters felt we would be able to get the majority of P-40's to Casablanca by that time.

Five of us in the Squadron were assigned this task. We all looked forward to this assignment. Most of us had combat experience and at one time or another secretly dreamed about flying the venerable P-40.

Our dreams finally came true as we all made a trip down to the area to see how the mechanics were doing on bringing the old ships back from the dead. Only a few mechanics would be assigned this detail and it meant that everyone would really be pushing hard to get all the ships to Casablanca in the assigned time. Little did we realize what we were getting into.

The first flight of ships was assembled and ready to go and so were we. Getting our briefing and weather, we decided that Tunis, North Africa would be the first gas stop. Before climbing into the P-40's, we made a visual inspection and were aghast at the deplorable condition of these ships. We had been used to flying the brand new P-51's, P-38's, P-47's, etc., and now down to this. Well it was for a good cause, we told ourselves.

After a quick conference to compare notes, we decided yes, they were basically all in that same sad deplorable condition. We all asked ourselves the same question, "What did we do to deserve this awful assignment?"

My particular ship was in shambles, I felt extremely uncomfortable in trying to fly this, "Hunk of Junk," over the Mediterranean, then across miles and miles of desert to arrive at the final destination, Casablanca. A total of over five hours of rugged water and terrain flying, and for what? Being young and eager to help in the war effort, we all agreed to give it our best try.

Lining up on the runway, we checked out the engines and took off on a south heading. It was decided to follow the Italian coast line just in case of trouble. Flying a loose formation we soon found out that half the radios did not work. Three ships turned back for mechanical reasons. I was one of the three as my engine was running so rough I had real trouble getting this crate safely back down. After my return, I soon found out that none of the five had even gotten as far as Sicily.

The next day the same scenario was repeated. This time one guy was forced to bail out off the coast of Italy and only one ship made the coast of Africa. Another made an emergency landing in Southern Italy. That makes ten out of ten that did not make Casablanca. Only one out of ten made Tunis.

The third try we were all definitely getting very gun-shy. As I pulled up to the flight line the standing joke was, "How far today, Sir?"

"God knows," I replied. Realizing that our secret dream had turned to a nightmare.

The Curtiss P-40 similar to the one in the chapter of *"The Boondoggle."*
(Photo courtesy U.S. Air Force Museum.)

"Don't worry Sir, this one is the best of the bunch, it's an F-model and I will personally guarantee that it's just like a new ship," said my mechanic. For the first time since this program began, I felt maybe just maybe, I might get this one to Casablanca.

It was a very beautiful morning and as I checked out the ship and engine, I felt confident that maybe today we would be lucky and get all five down to Casablanca. After all, we had littered the flight areas with a lot of P-40's, and once down they usually stayed there for good.

It was the standard practice to keep the canopy open for all take-offs and landings, the reason being it would be much easier for the rescue crew to get to you if something should happen.

On every P-40 we flew, the rudder did a massage job on your feet and legs. Lifting up the tail would get rid of this problem, and then the ship flew smoothly, with no rudder pedal vibrations. Pushing the stick forward the ship picked up speed rapidly. Tail up the ship leaped into the air, eager for flight.

I reached down, pulled the lever for the gear retraction, and started my climb out.

About this time there was a tremendous explosion and a very hot blast of glycol completely covered the windshield and cockpit. It burned my face and got under my goggles and into my eyes. I couldn't see a thing.

Pulling off the power, I tried to feel for the ground.

The next thing I knew, the ship hit the ground and I came to a dead stop, completely dazed and unable to see.

Witnesses said: "The ship pulled up in a stall and then fell off in a right turn spin. First the right wing, then the nose hit the ground." The ship stopped in a huge cloud of dust and white smoke. The ambulance sped me off to the hospital for medical aid. I was afriad that I might never see again.

Oh God, did my eyes burn and water!

The doctor at the hospital did a thorough exam and said, "Perhaps if you're lucky, you might get your sight back."

"What about flying again, Doc?" I asked.

"Hell son, you're lucky to be alive."

I was very happy several hours later, when I slowly recovered my eyesight. I knew then that I would soon be back up in the air.

Taking stock of this debacle, our Commander decided that enough is enough. Only two P-40's had made it safely to Casablanca and it was time now to put an end to this awful boon-doggle.

This was by no means the end of the boon-doggles. I had gone back to Casablanca about a month or so after this episode and signed out a brand new P-51-D for delivery to Pomigliano, Italy.

I had flown a lot of Mustangs in my career and I must admit this particular ship made a real impression on me. The minute I started the engine I fell madly in love. After checking out the ship around the pattern, I landed and contacted the line chief and said, "Man, this has got to be the best running and flying Mustang that I ever been in. I have never in all my life flown one that turns me on like this one, it's perfect."

"Glad to hear that, Sir," he says. "Should make some combat pilot very pleased."

As I made my way from Casablanca to Oran, Maison Blanche, then Tunis, I just couldn't help thinking. "Boy, what a ship, the pilot that winds up with this should be one happy guy." I was quite pleased to think that I would be bringing this one up, and could hardly wait to tell the operations officer what a good ship this would be for the Fighter Squadron. I left Tunis and Naples appeared all too soon. God, I sure hated to part with this Mustang. I've never ever felt this way about any other P-51, but this one was without a bit of doubt, the exception.

Landing at Pomigiano, I taxied up to the usual parking and tie down area. Hopping out, I was greeted by this non-flying Captain Winthroph. "How did your trip go?" he asked. "Fine," I replied. "Here is the airplane's Form 5. All I need now is a receipt to show I delivered it here."

"No problem," he said as he signed a document showing that I did turn over this ship to the proper department.

"Say, Captain, do you know what outfit might get this ship?"

"Why no, I don't," he said.

"Believe me, this is by far the best P-51 I have ever flown and . . ." I stopped talking and stared in disbelief. A tug had hooked up to my ship and towed it over towards an area that had a bunch of junked airplanes and parts laying all over the place.

"Just what the hell are those guys doing with my ship, Captain?" I said very irritated.

Before another word is spoken, two Italian men take an ax and punch a hole in the bottom of the wings. The gas flows out very quickly. Now they tow the ship another twenty feet or so and line it up with a huge metal guillotine. They work very rapidly and methodically. The blade comes down with a mightly whoosh! slicing off the engine from the firewall. Then the rest of the ship, minus engine, is pushed over to the side as it joins the rest of the remains of many other ships.

"WHY? WHY?" I asked.

"We just have too many airplanes here now," said the Captain, "and my orders are to reduce this number immediately."

I just can't understand this. But, there's no doubt about it. I am once again involved in another . . . *Boon-doggle* . . .

Savage (left) and Tapp (right) in front of the Capodichino Airdrome, Naples, Italy.

Chapter 16
Almost Tapps For Tapp

Roland Tapp and I had been through a lot together, training, combat and now the Overseas Ferry Command. Both of us had many enjoyable hours of flying on each other's wing. We knew how to work as a team and there was little doubt that we both loved to fly.

The schedule for this day was for each of us to lead a flight of four P-47 Thunderbolts from Tunis, North Africa on up to Naples, Italy.

Prior to this flight, Roland approached me early this morning and said, "Say, Doc, keep an eye on me when we fly out over the water, OK?"

I said, "What for?"

"Well," said Roland, "I have been getting a little bit of vertigo the last few times when flying over the water, and I thought I had better talk to you about it."

"Aw, you'll be OK," I assured him, "but don't worry, I'll be nearby in case you need me." With these few words, an adventure was about to unfold that would without a doubt live in both of our minds forever.

Our plans were to have Roland and his flight take off first, and I and my group would follow directly behind. We planned to assemble over the land area of Tunis, prior to taking off over the Med for Naples.

The flight plan called for a direct flight to Naples, which generally took an hour and a half, using Sicily as the mid-point of our trip. In fact, we would just barely see the western edge of Sicily if we were on course.

Roland and I had learned over the past year how easy it was for a single engine ship to go automatic rough the minute land would disappear. We had thoroughly briefed our young 2nd Lt's on this fact and felt that it would not be a major problem today.

As I ran up the Thunderbolt, my mind kept flashing back to what Roland had told me earlier. Naw, there is really nothing wrong, I assured myself as I swung into position for take off. Roland by now was airborne with his flight of four, circling above the area waiting for me to join up with my flight.

We made contact first by radio and then visually as we formed up and flew a loose two-flight eight ship formation. As was usual, just the minute land vanished, we both had a couple of calls, saying that they (P-47 wingmen) were experiencing rough engines. We calmed them down by saying, "Take it easy, your engine will start running smooth again."

Sure enough, they came back on the air in a few minutes with, "Everything appears to be OK now."

I called Roland and said, "How are you doing?"

"So far, so good," was his reply. Today was another day of haze and no horizon. Climbing up through 10,000 feet I felt we should be topping out the haze at any time. Due to this thick haze we had to fly instruments the minute we went out over the water. I was quite unprepared for the next call, when a voice on the radio said: *"Hey Doc! I'm in real deep trouble!"* it was Roland and he did sound different.

"What's your problem?" I called out.

"I can't control my ship and I'm going to crash," he said.

"That's nuts and you know it," I snapped back.

"I'm serious and it's for real," said Rollo. By now I really got the feeling that Roland was in trouble.

"Roger, I know there is no horizon today," I assured him, "but just fly your instruments and you'll be OK," I assure him.

"I can't! I'm losing it!" came his quick reply.

"Damn it, the hell you can't! Stick in there, you'll be OK," I shouted back at him.

Now I can tell that Roland is getting more desperate as a couple of his wingmen say it's getting hard to stay with him because of his erratic flying.

I called my no. 2 wingman and say, "Take over the flight and go on up to Naples." Then next telling his no. 2 wingman, "Take over Roland's flight and join up with the other guys." Now I can concentrate on Roland by not having to worry about six other P-47's. By this time I see Roland diving and then climbing erratically. "Hang on, Roland; I'm coming!" I yell. This doesn't do any good as his maneuvers seem to be getting worse. I finally pull up alongside his right wing and tuck in as close as I can, "OK Roland, I am right next to you. Look to your right, do you hear me? *Look to your right!*"

I was tucked in so tight to him, that when he finally looks out towards me I can see deep concern on his face. "What the hell's wrong with you?" I ask.

"I don't know, I can't seem to fly straight, and I'm real dizzy," he said.

"Roger, it's probably because you don't have a decent horizon," I reply. "Stay with me now and I'll get you down closer to the water for a horizon."

Now with his eyes glued on me he said, "OK, Doc."

Slowly, ever so slowly, starting down, I am able to gradually lose altitude to where we are now about 500 feet above the water.

"Not much of a horizon, but at least I can see the white caps on the water now," I say to Roland.

"All right look outside Roland, you should be OK."

Relaxing his attention away from me, he looked out and almost immediately went into a steep climbing left turn back up into the haze and instrument conditions. "*What's wrong?*" I yelled.

"*I'm still dizzy and feel like I'm going to puke,*" said Roland in a real weak voice.

"Hang in there, I'll be flying on your right wing again, as soon as I can catch you," I radioed back.

"*I don't know if I can,*" came Roland's answer.

God damn it, you've got to, I'll be right next to you," I replied. Pushing the throttle to full power I was finally able to fly back on to his wing. I thought for a minute or two that I would lose him as he was wandering all over the sky.

Again I had to go through the same procedure, but this time he stuck to me just like glue. "Keep talking to me." I pleaded, as I slowly worked our way towards Catania, Sicily. Finally we got close enough to the air base and I was able to call the Tower and advised them of our problem. I care-

fully worked our two ships down to the pattern altitude and advised Roland,
"OK, the runway is in sight, you can land now."

"Roger, was his weak reply. Then he said, "No I can't."

"Why not," I said.

"*Because I'm too sick and I can't,*" he replied.

"OK, then I'll try and fly right down to the runway and you can take
over from there," I said.

"*Roger, Roger,*" came his weak reply.

The tower had heard everything and understood. They then gave us
permission to make this most unorthodox approach. Meanwhile Roland
was stuck to me and my P-47 like we were one. As we approached the runway I worked him down to about fifty feet and said:

"Drop your gear and flaps, NOW!

Look out now you're right over the runway. Chop your power and
LAND!"

He did not want to look out, but reluctantly agreed.

Looking at the runway, he finally made contact.

Then POW . . . POW . . . POW . . . each time he bounced just a little
bit higher. I thought, My God! he is going to lose it after all this.

Finally, his ship stopped as I flew by overhead. Banking to the left, I
tried to watch his every move. The ambulance met him as his ship rolled to
a wobbly stop.

The Tower came on the air with, "Congratulations, well done." I then
flew on to Naples alone. I later found out that he was very dizzy and unable
to stand. The minute he attempted to step out on the wing, he fell forward
and started to vomit violently.

The doctor's at the Base Hospital finally diagnosed his problem as
Meniere's Disease of the inner ears. He spent the next nine months in Air
Force Hospitals and after that was put on the Air Force disability retired
list.

Army "Grasshopper" typical of the one flown in the chapter "*Luck of the Draw*".
Owner: Max Marion

Chapter 17
Luck Of The Draw

An urgent message had been received in Ferry headquarters from Metz, France. They requested as many new recon ships as we had, to be delivered ASAP. It was more of a plea than a request. The Battle of the Bulge had begun and we were getting our butts clobbered. There was a dire shortage of photo recon ships for reporting enemy troop movements and they needed the ships desperately.

I was assigned the task of leading a flight of four P-51 photo recon's from Casablanca, North Africa up to Metz, France. I had never been in France before, and was anxious to see some new country.

We carefully checked our ships out prior to this really long cross-country flight. It would be close to seven hours of flying according to the flight planning charts. Before our departure, I met with the other pilots and decided that we would fly a loose four-ship formation, to help keep us from getting too tired. Barring any delays, I figured we would be in Metz in about two days or three at the latest.

Our flight plan was filed from Casablanca . . . Oran . . . and Tunis with an RON (remain overnight).

From Tunis, we would fly to Naples, Italy, Marseilles, and Lyon, France, then finally depending on the weather, Metz.

By and large, it was an uneventful trip. Fortunately, the weather broke enough for us to make it in two days. As I led my formation over the airport at Metz, the weather here was overcast and spitting light snow. SNOW? We were stationed in North Africa and hadn't seen snow in almost two years.

Landing at the makeshift airstrip, the snow depth was startling with four or more feet in drifts. We taxied up to the parking area and were met by armed guards with helmets, boots, white gloves, and side arms. That's pretty neat but maybe a bit overdone we thought, as we signed off our ships to the Squadron C.O.

"By the way," said the C.O. "What outfit are you guys in?"

"The Air Force," we piped back.

"You can't be," came his reply, "you're not dressed for it."

We had just left North Africa's 90 degrees in Khaki's and "T" shirts . . . summer flying togs and, of course, we had well sun tanned bodies. Next to our white-face counterparts, there was actually no comparison. We did not fit the Fighter pilot profile of this area.

It took a lot of talk to persuade the guys, yes, we really are pilots in the U.S. Air Force. They were finally convinced, but left us with a very real strong warning.

"This is Patton's country and you had better get your shit together. This means in proper uniform. Helmet, winter clothes, side arms, white gloves and putties, or you will be subject to a $75 fine."

Due to the crazy weather the C-47 shuttle had been delayed and wasn't due in for two days. TWO DAYS! How can we last two days in this area? We didn't have the right type of clothes for the General or this cold country.

I could hardly believe my ears. "How can an Army General dictate to the Air Force?" I ask. (The military had decided a while back that the Air Force would be separate from the Army. So the Army Air Corps name has now been officially changed to the U.S. Air Force.)

"No matter," replied one of the local pilots, "His orders apply to all."

We found the BOQ (Bachelor Officers Quarters) and grabbed supper. That night in the bar at the club, we heard that two ships known as Grass-hoppers, or Piper Cubs were scheduled to depart tomorrow for Lyon, France. What an incredible piece of luck. That's exactly where we had to go, in order to pick up another shuttle ride back home to Casablanca.

Since I was the CO, I couldn't bring myself to pull rank. So . . . I decided, "OK, we'll cut the cards and the two high cards will be the lucky ones to get out the next morning."

"Fair enough," was the reply, and with the cards shuffled, the draw began. Quite naturally we drew a large crowd as there was a lot at stake here.

I pulled the first card. It was the King of hearts. Now the tensions began to mount as the other cards were drawn. Next came the ten of Diamonds, followed by two lower cards. This established just who would be able to go, and who had to stay. Everyone agreed it was a fair deal.

After all the excitement died down the four of us decided that we would stay a little longer at the club. After all, we two lucky ones had to celebrate. It's been pure luck that we stumbled on these guys. Now two of us at least, will be able to get out of this damn cold area. It turned out to be quite a party at the local Officer's Club, despite all the drinking and fun we were constantly reminded that, "Just remember guys, you're out of uniform and subject to a fine if they catch you."

In our present condition we all joked and said, "They've got to catch us first."

"Oh, don't worry, they will," replied several voices at the bar. With that dire warning, we decided it's time to retire to the sack. Two of us faced an early morning flight.

The next day the weather cleared and the two of us were introduced to our pilots, both were Flying Sergeants.

My pilot had heard that I was a former fighter pilot and really made a point of telling me how pleased he was to fly me and my partner back to Lyon, France.

As we approached the two ships, I was shocked to see just how small these craft appeared and so much like a model paper airplane. The Sergeant queried me on my combat experiences and made quite a point in telling me how he planned to show us just exactly the way they flew in combat.

Putting me in the front seat, he shoved this map at me and said, "Here, you navigate."

That was fine by me, but I failed to take in consideration that my mind was still locked on flying a P-51, and at these slow speeds my navigation was way ahead of that little ship.

Taking off in formation, we immediately went back down on the deck, flying around trees, over buildings, and under power lines. I hadn't counted on doing this type of air navigation.

Everything was looking the same and after a while, I tapped him on the shoulder and shouted, "I'm not sure where we are!"

"No matter," he replied. "I know this area real well." About an hour had elapsed when he turned to me and yelled: "Do you know where we are?" I shook my head no. I had absolutely no idea.

"Give me the map," he yelled again. After a few minutes, he then shouted, "Damn. I'm not sure either! But we will ask them."

He climbed his little ship up to about 500 ft. The other Grasshopper pulled up alongside of us. Pointing to his map, he gave a look of: "I'm lost," and "Where are we gesture," with his hands.

The other pilot raised his arms and shook his head with, "I don't know."

"That's OK," he yelled to me, "This happens all the time." I was more relaxed flying at this higher altitude, but quite concerned now about being lost.

As we flew over a ridge and trees, a large soccer field came into view. "How about that!" he shouted with obvious joy. Banking around the field he lined up to the east for a landing. The other ship was right on our tail as we dove over some trees that were on the approach end of the field. The dive increased our speed to the point where it looked for certain we would overshoot the field.

Now the trees on the far side were looming up fast and I knew for sure we would crash.

Crossing both arms in front of my face I waited for the worst.

The next thing I heard was the snapping of tree limbs as the wheels went through them. Incredible! We're still flying?

Climbing for altitude I open my eyes and can actually see a few branches that have literally wrapped themselves around our gear as a re- minder of just how close we came to buying the farm.

I noticed that the other ship had landed successfully. We lined up again for still another try, finally touching down the last half of the field much too fast.

Good God! I can't believe it. This dumb son-of-a-bitch is landing down-wind. We proceeded to go beyond the boundry and on out to the ad- joining road followed by a hard half-right turn, still following the road. Finally we came to a stop on the road.

He does a one-eighty on the road and taxies back to the field. Finally, parking his ship next to the other ship. WHEW!!! I was still shaking as I climbed out of the ship.

All four of us got together and checked the map. No one had absolutely the faintest idea as to where we were.

About this time we could see a dozen or so kids running from the school playground towards us. My pilot said confidently, "No problem, I'll talk to them. I can speak French."

A blond girl about 12 years old came out of the group and he spoke to her in French asking her to point on the map just exactly where we are.

She replied, "Nein, sprechen zie Deutsch." Pointing to the map, she showed us that we were almost 50 miles inside Germany.

Our legs turned to jelly as we weakly made our way to the ships. I was so mad I threatened to have this character court-marshalled for doing such a stupid-ass stunt. After 35 missions and almost a year in combat, I felt this would be one hell of a way to get killed or even wind up as a POW.

"How can anyone ever explain this?" I asked him. I was so mad and hot under the collar I found it hard to remain civil and talk in a calm voice.

The other ship immediately fired up and took off leaving us all alone. My pilot asked me to prop the ship. I tried and tried but could not get it to even pop. We were totally alone now, as the kids had left along with the other ship.

Fear and imagination had really set in and I was soaking wet from this and the total physical exhaustion trying to hand-prop this little engine. Swearing constantly, I couldn't help keep myself from threatening him over and over again with a court-martial. That is, if we both get out of this thing alive. These threats didn't help one bit.

As the time passes, my imagination begins to work. I actually believe I can see German soldiers lining up on the ridge pointing their rifles at us just waiting and ready to blow us away.

Deciding that maybe he would have better luck, we changed positions and tried again. Still no go.

After what seemed like forever, the little engine gave a small pop, then another small pop. A small ray of hope, as it popped again.

With the next pull, it finally sprang to life. He hopped in the pilot's seat, gave it full throttle and blasted off out of this field. No time for a mag check this time.

After a few miles we climbed up to a respectable altitude of 4,000 feet and made an uneventful trip back to Lyon, France. By the time we had landed, I had cooled off enough to the point I would not press my charges. I was just glad to be here and alive.

I wound up giving him a thorough lecture about such a stupid ass stunt like that.

His final departing statement was a quiet and somber,

"YES SIR! . . . NO SIR! . . . GOOD-BY SIR!"

C-47, similar to the ship that was delayed in picking us up at Metz. (Photo courtesy U.S. Air Force.)

Savage with the 328th Ferry Squadron's B-25, Capodichino Airport, Naples, Italy, 1944.

Chapter 18
Booze-Beer

The 328th Ferry Squadron had been very busy bringing up all the many new P-39's that were arriving almost daily at the Casablanca depot. It was a constant surprise to us every time we came back to Casa not knowing what type of ship we would be flying next week.

The last boat load brought in the latest P-39-Q models. I first fell in love with the P-39 when I was in cadets. Without a doubt, I was looking forward to flying them now. Little did I realize how much I would be hating these ships in just a few short weeks from now. They would constantly boil over long before we could even get them airborne, but this was only one out of a series of many problems.

None of us liked the idiot's delight as we called it. Both the manifold, mixture and prop control, were on one throttle lever. Literally and figuratively, this stupid gadget gave us fits. Nothing ever seemed to work right. We were glad we only had two hundred to deliver.

When we first got these ships, we had to sit out in the hot sun at the end of the runway waiting for them to cool in order to take-off. Later we learned to get our take-off clearance first, before we started the engine.

Then we would go hell-bent-for election to the end of the runway and take-off without stopping. We checked the mags by placing one hand on the panel to stop the shaking, in order to steady it for a reading.

Several months later, orders were received for us to give these ships to the Russians. They loved the '39 as a tank buster with its nose cannon. Apparently it was a great *cold weather ship! It sure wasn't worth a shit in this part of the country.*

I was scheduled to fly this ship to Tunis and then on to Naples. This was the general collection area prior to our delivery to the various Fighter Squadrons.

We made it a standard practice never to fly alone on these delivery trips, especially with the P-39's. The only exception to this was when we flew a twin engine ship. I was in complete agreement with this policy. We always flew with a minimum of two or more on the trip across North Africa and over the Med.

Our flight course took us over the mountains, desert and a large body of water. Almost every flight condition imaginable was encountered. It just made good sense flying together. In fact it was a standing order from headquarters, in addition we were required to file and close flight plans.

It was here I began to see where the meteorologist started to put forth some new neat stuff. They developed a three dimension type profile chart that helped us get a pictorial view of just what we might expect on our flights. Unfortunately, the only weather stations were strategically located at the major ports of Oran, Maison Blanche, and Tunis. There was always a lot of unknown weather that no one ever knew about.

Today after checking the weather, I decided to fly just a two ship formation from Casablanca to Tunis. We usually always flew at a very high altitude to beat the intense heat that was so common for this time of the year. Climbing up and leveling off at 12,000 feet, we were rapidly approaching one of the highest terrain points of our trip, the Meknes Pass. This large mountain chain separated the North African coast line from the fierce harsh desert.

This pass was rather high at 8,000 feet, but we would have plenty to spare at our altitude. It was bleak and stark. Yet it was quite an elegant and beautiful sight. One can't help wonder just what those poor people on the ground must do to make their way around such a huge obstruction. Then after you get through the pass, all that remains is, ugh! that horrible desert, where very few things are found alive.

Suddenly I am snapped out of my serenity as the engine begins to miss a beat. I radioed my partner advising him that my ship is started to act up a bit.

The P-39 Bell "Aircobra" similar to the ones in the chapter of "*Booze Beer*".
(Photo courtesy U.S. Air Force Museum.)

"Hey Doc! Quit kidding around. Now is not the time for that," says Chuck Leedham.

"No kidding," I say, but I'm not too concerned, as I feel that the engine probably will clear up momentarily.

How wrong I am. Now it is starting to get much worse. I call Chuck again, and say, "Hey, this is no joke Chuck, it looks like I'm getting into a real problem with this dude."

"Roger. Do you think you can make it back to Casa?" shot back Chuck.

"Not really, I am starting to lose altitude and unable to get this gal to run very good," I replied. "I have tried everything that I can think of including changing the fuel selectors. I have no choice, *either bail out or go down!*"

After checking my charts, I found an airport located on the very edge of the desert. This was confirmed about the same time by my wingman and buddy Chuck. I call him and say, "It looks like my best plan would be to land down there, but be sure and wait until I am down safely before you go on."

"Roger on that," was his immediate response.

I slowly let down and circled over this airport checking out everything very carefully prior to landing. The airport appeared to be just fine. I spotted the wind sock and swung into the wind for a landing. Calling back to Chuck, I asked him if he would be sure to notify Squadron Headquarters in Casablanca of my plight, adding, "I only hope I can get out of here in a few days."

Taxing up to the parking area, the engine is running quite rough and I am very happy to be on the ground. I'm shocked to find there is absolutely no one around. Could this be one of those abandoned airports we all have heard about? Holy cow, what if I can't get word to anyone, what will happen?" I ask myself. By now, Chuck has long since vanished over the horizon.

As I swung the ship around on the parking area, I had a real funny feeling in the pit of my stomach. It was very hot, and I had no water on my ship or any supplies, other than a very small candy bar. A candy bar in this desert? What a joke! I'm sure that it would make me that much thirstier.

I ask myself silently, "OK, Doc. What if you can't find water on this old airport?"

I was really starting to talk aloud to myself. "Come on now, it can't be all that bad," I said. But with no one around, I found that I was, without a doubt beginning to get a mite concerned.

I walked over to the old administration building hoping that I would see someone. *No one, absolutely no one!* Looking around the old abandoned hangars I wondered how long it had been since man was on this field.

About a half hour had elapsed since I landed. I began to feel panic starting to set in, when I noticed a big cloud of dust and what appeared to be a truck in the distance. Was this a mirage or for real?

I have heard something about this at one time or the other, when a person may seem to think he really sees something. In reality it could be miles and miles away, or maybe nothing at all. The hot desert sun along with the heat plays a lot of tricks.

Closer examination proved it to be one of our old 6 by 6 Army trucks flying an American flag from its cab. Stopping the truck in a cloud of dust, I was greeted by a Major White who was dressed in the typical Army summer uniform. Driving this truck was an Army sergeant. Both identified themselves as the last of the rear guard element that had been assigned to this area.

The Major said he was a doctor and the Army had ordered him to stay there to help the civilians. Naturally, my first request was for some water. They were more than happy to oblige, and informed me that I was the first American that they had seen in over ten months. They were starved for news and I was treated like a celebrity.

As I was talking to them bringing them up to date on the happenings of the war, we all noticed what appeared to be a B-17 circling over the airport with one of its four engines in the feathered position. "Boy, that's incredible," said the Major. "We haven't seen anyone for so long and look at what we have now. Boy! we can all have a big party now."

Parking next to my sick P-39, the B-17 crew deplane from their crippled ship.

Introducing ourselves, we all felt quite fortunate that we were able to find this airport and help. In order to make us feel more at home, the Major said, "We have room for everyone at headquarters."

Climbing aboard the 6 by 6, we made our dusty way down the road to the headquarters of this American outpost. Inside everything is quite informal, as the Major pours a drink for all that want it. Whiskey that is. "Water is quite precious, and has to be carefully monitored," he says, as another big round of drinks are set up. "Out here our big concerns are not about rank, says the Major. That's OK by most of the men, including the officers of the B-17.

"Oh, by the way, did you guys happen to see the big white walled city as we drove in?" said the Major.

"Yeah, sure did," replied several men.

"Got to admit, it looked pretty modern for being way out here in the edge of the desert," I said.

"After dinner, I have a surprise for you guys," said the Major. "Incidentally, for your information, the airport that you used was one of the airports that the French Foreign Legion used prior to this war. They plan to reactivate it just as soon as the war ends."

"Well, getting back to the white-walled city; called Bose Bier," said the Major, "it's called the city of a thousand whores." Several of the men gave a loud whistle.

Then the Major continues, "Gentlemen, in case you haven't noticed, I am a doctor, and I would advise you all not to get involved, as these girls have diseases that we don't even know about. But, I think it would be nice to show you the sights.

Remember, look, but don't touch!"

Arriving at this one enormous house, we were greeted by an English-speaking woman who hailed from Brooklyn, New York. She introduced herself as: "I'm the madam here and welcome you all to my house and my friends. We are here to entertain and be of service to you. I'm affectionately known as: '*The Madam of the American House.*' "

Walking in, we are truly taken aback by the grandeur of the place. A huge mahogany bar, mirrors, liquors of every brand and description, and a very plush red rug.

"Well fellows, name your poison," she says.

It's incredible. I haven't seen so many brands of liquor since I left the States almost three years ago. She is a very friendly person and in no time flat made us feel right at home.

At the clap of her hands a string of girls appeared out of no where. "Remember," the Major cautions, "I meant every word that I said." Her girls are real characters, and only a couple of them can speak some English. They are from everywhere: French; Greek; Italian; Egyptian; and Arabic.

We were all quite sure about the outcome. Meanwhile, I felt that now would be the time to get some answers to questions I have always wondered about.

"What made you come way out here from the States to run a place like this?" I ask.

"Money, and lots of it," adding, "and an easy way of life."

"What happens to one of your girls if she happens to get pregnant," asks another guy.

"No problem, we have a Catholic Nuns' house nearby and we give the baby to them. But, it is a rare occasion when this happens," she says. Incredible! There is absolutely no question that she won't answer.

"What keeps your girls from getting those vereal diseases we have all heard about!" pipes up one of the men.

"You have nothing to worry about," says our hostess from Brooklyn, "my girls are clean."

She realizes that there is no way the men will take the girls. Finally she says, "But fellows, these girls are here just for you. This is solely for the Americans: *This is an exclusive American House, reserved for Americans.*"

Looking around one can see hats of every branch of the U.S. services including dog tags, pictures and even shirts with all kinds of rank on them.

The particular girl she assigned to me was a small Arab not much more than 17 years old. She did her damndest to get me to go up to the room. *But, no way!*

We all finally decided that it was about time for us to leave this exclusive American House. Paying our bill we thanked the Madam.

As we departed the house and boarded our truck we couldn't help but notice a bearded Arab, on a jackass, being welcomed to what is now known as the . . . *Exclusive Arabian House!*

The Martin B-26. Generally knowns as "The Baltimore Whore" (no visible means of support.) Similar to the one ferried from Sardinia to Telergma, No. Africa, in the chapter from *"Telergma Terror Trip"*. (Photo courtesy U.S. Air Force Museum.)

Chapter 19
Telergma Terror Trip

Telergma is an Air Force training center airport located in the central part of North Africa. It was the staging and training area for pilots in from the states. They were assigned here for some additional combat training to help bring them up to combat readiness by instructors who had been previously involved in combat.

The Ferry Squadron was making a lot of trips to this facility bringing in ships that had been retired from combat. These ships in turn were reconditioned and overhauled then put back into the pool for training purposes. Usually the pilots stayed only about 2-3 weeks before shipping on out to a combat unit.

I had just flown in a Martin B-26 "Maurauder," more commonly known to us as the Baltimore Whore. (No visible means of support) from the island of Sardinia. The ship was nice to fly if everything went normal. This model had seen over eight months of combat and was in poor shape. Tongue-in-cheek I checked it out prior for the flight to Telergma. It just barely did check out. Everything of any value had been taken and a lot of older parts were substituted in their place. Despite the ratty condition and looks it did fly rather well.

Arrival at Telergma was uneventful and with the completion of the paper work, I went over to the BOQ and checked in for the night. They served a real good supper for a change and I looked forward to getting back to my home base the next day.

I awoke once during the night to hear the constant drumming of rain and sleet on the roof. "Rats, I hope this won't delay my trip back today," I said silently to myself.

Arising about seven, I went over to the flight operations to check weather. The metro officer said, "It is bad and the prog charts show it would probably stay like this way for at least 2 maybe 3 days."

I left and went on down to the Officers Mess hall for breakfast. I visited with a lot of pilots and found the crew who were supposed to leave today for Maison Blanche. Comparing notes, we all agreed that there would be no flights out today as far as they were concerned.

The second day was a repeat of the first. The third day wasn't much better. This became extremely discouraging for me as once again I was listed as a passenger on the scheduled departure flight. No American pilot wanted to leave under these weather conditions. By now the old dispatcher's temper was growing shorter.

I was told, "You're next on the list to depart."

But I really do not want to go as all of our pilots have again scrubbed flying for today," I said to the dispatcher.

"Well, not all of the pilots and ships. We have you scheduled out on a RAF Dakota, and if you decline, I'll leave you here for a week," he said.

With this threat hanging over my head, I reluctantly climbed on board the RAF ship. We had a full load and as the young commander came on board, I wondered just how he felt so damn confident that he could fly and make it.

It was still raining and quite foggy as we taxiied out for take-off. Seated next to me was this ground-pounder Major. A nice enough sort of a guy although visibly nervous. He started talking to me right away saying, "You're a pilot, right?"

"Yes Sir, how did you guess?" I replied.

''I see your're carrying a parachute,'' he replied. I had my A-2 flight jacket on with the chute lodged at my feet. "Well, at least this guy seems to be friendly," I thought, but dumb. He didn't even see the silver wings on my shirt.

We hadn't been airborne more than five minutes when I notice that he had stopped talking and was just staring out the window. Looking out the window there was little to see, only fog and rain. You could barely see the wing tip lights reflecting in the fog.

About a half hour into the flight, we started to hit some very rough air. The flight got into some real up and down drafts to the point it was more than just extremely rough. In fact, it was damned uncomfortable. Once again this strong feeling that I wished I had stayed back in Telergma came back on me. I tried talking to this major hoping to calm any fears he might have had. Perhaps I must have shown a bit of fear in my voice as it quivered and got very dry.

The major got very white and was sweating profusely. He turned to me and said, "I need some fresh air," and then promptly puked all over me. I had a hard enough time not joining him as I fought back that same horrible feeling.

I silently said, "As a pilot I just can't and won't let myself get that way." Fortunately, I was able to get my chute out of the way before that deluge hit, but man, I sure was a mess.

Feeling better, the major took out his handkerchief and tried to help me clean up the mess. I'm constantly fighting back that same nauseous feeling that I too was about ready to join him, not so much now from the mess and smell but from the horrible fear that I'm convinced we're not going to make it.

Adding further to this fear, I look out the window and can only see rocks and more rocks almost at our wingtip level.

"My God! what is this jerk trying to do?" I say.

"What do you mean?" said the major.

"Nothing," I said, trying not to alarm any of the passengers.

Suddenly we make another sharp turn to the left and I felt a tremendous "G" load pressure. Looking out our window, we can see the ground less than ten feet from our wing tip. The wing is actually waving up and down. Beads of sweat started to pop out on my head as I tried to restrain myself and remain calm. We came out of the bank as suddenly as we went in.

"I wonder what the hell kind of a maneuver that was?" said the major.

"It's known as a 180 degree turn, or let's get the hell out of here," I said.

Again we noticed the pilot starting up another valley. "I just don't believe it," I said, "he can't possibly be going to try it again?" "Try what?" asks the major. I completely ignore him as the ship flies in a straight line for the first time. About ten miles up this valley we ran into a dense fog bank and rain and went through the same type of gymnastic maneuver to get back out.

"Well, twice is a charm," I said, "I hope by now that this pilot has learned his lesson."

"Me, too," chimes in the major. I am so visibly shaken that my arms and legs are convulsing uncontrollably.

The major says, "You're a pilot, are we going to be OK?" Now how the hell would I know, much less be able to tell this major? I tried to calmly, but not very convincingly, assure him. "Yeah, we should make it."

Once more we start up another canyon. "We just can't continue to be this lucky," I said, wishing that I had not been so stupid to allow myself to be forced on this dumb RAF Dakota. After all, our pilots had sense enough not to go and had absolutely refused. Entering this third canyon will certainly be the end of us.

Each time we entered these blind canyons we just get out by the skin of our teeth. How lucky can anyone get? I tried to remain calm, but when it is completely out of your control, like this, it's almost hopeless.

Plunging ahead, I can only see the same scenario being played over and over again. Can we luck out a third time and get away with it? I strained to see out the side window just waiting for the inevitable crash, my life felt like it had come to a complete standstill.

Just about the time I had given up hope, the pilot suddenly pulled up in a steep climb, and all at once we were out in the other valley in the sunshine.

The landing at Maison Blanche was really anti-climactic. Getting out of the ship, I was a mess. I just couldn't resist waiting and personally talking to the captain of this ship. Coming out of the cockpit was a kid not much older than me and just as shaken as I. This trip really showed on him. I started to say, "Man, that was one hell of a ride . . ." but he cut me short by saying, "Damn glad we were so lucky and made it down safely, eh! Yank?"

Savage departing from Casablanca with new P-51-D.

Chapter 20
The Luftwaffe Ace

Three of us had been assigned the task of flying P-38's from Casablanca to Foggia, Italy. The weather in North Africa had been ideal and I was scheduled to lead my three ship formation across North Africa up to the Fighter base in Foggia.

We all felt quite lucky that we were assigned this task. The P-38 was a neat ship to fly and I thoroughly enjoyed the beautiful soft sounds of its engines, particularly when you taxied it. In flight, it had a different sound than the rest of the fighters, it was like that of a twin Chris-Craft motor boat, and it really hummed as it flew along.

Doing our usual walk-around, pre-flight, and check list, we had found nothing unusual about any of the three ships. These particular units had just recently been built in the United States, were pickled and then placed on a freighter cargo ship that sailed across the sub-infested Atlantic Ocean to Casablanca.

After reassembly, they were then test-flown and made ready for the ferry flight that would eventually take them several thousand miles to the front for active duty service. Most of the time we had no problems, but every once in a while some major problem would develop. There was no such thing as a piece of cake mission, it was extremely important to be constantly vigilant.

The flight departed Casablanca and as we flew over the Mekness Pass, I remember it wasn't too many months ago that I had an emergency there. Flying on to Oran, Algiers, and Tunis went without a hitch. Despite the fact we had good tailwinds, it was decided that because of the bad weather hammering Italy, we would RON, (Remain Over Night) in Tunis and try for Italy the next day.

Getting up early, we checked the weather for our route of flight and destination. Accurate weather info was always scarce except for our midway point Sicily, and our final destination, Foggia. I had selected Naples as our alternate. Getting my flight assembled we all went to the mess hall for chow.

Meanwhile, I had ordered the ships fueled and we were on our way before 9 AM. The trip went without incident and was very pleasant. Fortunately, the foul weather that had plagued Italy was just now starting to move out as we arrived over the Fighter field. I called their Tower for field conditions and landing instructions.

The makeshift Tower replied and advised, "Active runway is 090 degrees and landing is to the East.

Be advised that due to all the recent rains, the strip is very soft and there are many areas of standing water."

"Roger," I replied.

With this word of caution, I decided that we would carefully check out the strip by giving it a good visual prior to making a decision as to whether we would, or would not, land.

On the first pass, I could hardly believe my eyes. It actually looked like a small lake with a bunch of little islands. All three of us made a pass and then rendezvoused above the strip. We could see all the Group's P-38's parked in the revetments and no one else was flying except us.

One of the pilots in my flight said, "What do you think, Doc?"

I replied, "It doesn't look too good. I think it would be a smart idea if we all went on over to Naples." Almost all of the Fighter bases in Foggia were cut from farm fields and very few had hard surface runways.

"Maybe we ought to check it out one more time," came another voice.

"Roger," I said, "but you know it has been raining here for over a week, and I'm not too sure it would be a good idea attempting a landing now." Then I added, "Well, maybe we could try another low pass and really check closer this time before we definitely decide."

"Roger," "Roger," came the response from my other two wingmen who were tucked in on my right in a very tight right echelon formation.

Perhaps to show off a bit? Maybe.

Calling the Tower once more, we again advised them of our intentions. Down we came, this time with our landing gear and flaps fully extended. This would give us a much slower approach speed and a lot more time to check over the strip.

As we pulled back up, the Tower came back on the air with, "Gentleman, what are your intentions?"

Gear and flaps back up, we regrouped and I radioed back saying, "I feel that the strip is too wet and muddy to land these new ships."

"Roger, understand," came the voice from the Tower over our radios.

With the decision made, I called the other two ships to reform on me so we could fly back to Pomigliano, an airport near Naples where we had been putting all the extra ships that we could not deliver. This airport had several hard surface runways. In addition we were more familiar with the facilities and accommodations for the transient pilot.

About this time the radio crackled, "*Hello . . . Flight leader of the P-38's, come in, please.*"

I called back in response, "Roger, this is the P-38 leader, what is your request?"

"This is Colonel J. Jones, Commander of the Wing. We need those P-38 aircraft and would like you to deliver them NOW!"

"I understand, Sir, but I really feel that your airport is too wet and not safe to land," I radioed back.

"That's nonsense, I am the Base Commander, and I order you and your flight to land!"

"But . . . but . . . ," I started to say and hesitated.

"No buts about it, this is Colonel Jones, and, *that's an order.*"

"Yes Sir," I replied. We all lined up for our echelon formation and pitch up to the left, which was the standard procedure, for pattern and landing.

Despite his order, I was very apprehensive about landing here.

Lowering my landing gear and flaps once again, I said to our flight, "Well, here goes," as I started to land.

I touched down in a shower of water and mud, fearing to even put on my brakes as I slid to a very slippery stop. I barely managed to get turned around at the end of the strip. I then started taxiing back to the parking area and had one hell of a time keeping the airplane under control.

The Tower called and said, "The Colonel wants you to park your flight next to the C-47 by our base ops building."

"Roger, understand. Will do," I replied.

Little did I realize what would happen with this simple request.

Taxiing up towards the C-47, I had to apply considerable power to both engines in order for me to get the P-38 moving through the wet and extremely muddy field conditions.

As I got closer, I realized that I had absolutely no braking power at all due to the wet slippery conditions. Sliding slightly sideways, I elected to cut both of my engines as I gradually slid to a stop, but not before the nose guns of my P-38 had impacted the left wing of the C-47. The props had stopped, but now the left blade on my left engine had struck the left cowling of the C-47. I felt awful.

The Colonel came storming out just raising hell. *"Why didn't you use differential power? If you had used the power on on engine only, you could have missed the C-47!* he yelled.

Sorry, Sir, but I didn't want to land here to begin with, and made the decision only because of your orders, Sir. Not only that, if I did as you suggested, Sir, I feel that the damage could have been much worse, SIR."

It was pretty hard for a Colonel to admit that he was at fault for anything, but just about everyone there agreed that no one had flown from the field for over a week because of the dismal weather and sloppy conditions.

Even though I knew I was right, it still didn't make me feel any better to know that I had just become a Luftwaffe Ace as I logged the fourth and fifth American plane to my credit.

The P-38 "Pathfinder" similar to the one in the chapter of *"The Hitch Hiker"*. (Photo courtesy U.S. Air Force Museum.)

Chapter 21
The Hitch-Hiker

Activity around Capodichino Airport was at its peak. There were all types of service people trying to go somewhere. As a Ferry Squadron our trips were mostly one way with a pick up by our shuttle for a return flight back to our home base. Today I was assigned to take this P-38 Pathfinder over to a B-17 bomber group located just south of Foggia, Italy.

The B-17's used the Pathfinder with all its new type radar to help get them to their intended target. The Pathfinder was unique. It was just like a regular P-38 but had been converted for these very special missions.

On closer examination, it had a different nose configuration. The nose had been extended to accommodate all of the latest radar technologies available for that time. One of its key primary missions was to lead the bombers. Additionally it was designed to jam the very effective radar that was being used by the Germans to fire their anti-aircraft guns. This radar-directed flak was taking its deadly toll on the bombers. Finally . . . I think, we now have come up with a tool that could take out the enemy's guns lethal sting.

I had never flown this Pathfinder type and wondered if it would present any problem for me. After checking out the paper work, I went out to give it a good visual inspection. Everything was normal, and I decided why not look up inside the nose and try to check out some or all the gadgets.

Immediately below the nose is a trap door. I find that this trap door can be operated from the outside as well as inside. Opening the door and crawling up into the compartment, I then whistled aloud and said to myself, "Man oh man, that's a hell-of-a-lot of dials and stuff." Looking over all the equipment, I'm at a loss to even begin to know what it will do. "Well, that's not my problem," I mutter. Swinging into the seat I find that it's quite comfortable. Aha! here to my left is a head set that the navigator/bombardier can use to communicate with the pilot or even Bomber Command.

I wasn't on a tight schedule so I thought I would spend a little extra time completely looking over this ship. The nose was quite similar to the glass nose of the bombers. Glass covered three-quarters of the area and the visibility was absolutely terrific. I bet the guy riding up here would not miss a thing, as he has the front row seat to everything.

Could be a bit scary though when the action starts.

Climbing down and out of the nose compartment I started back toward operations for a final check on any possible last minute details that might have to be taken care of. Walking out of base operations, I was met by a highly decorated major. His uniform with the crossed rifles told me that he was in the infantry. The shoulder patch indicated he was in the 5th Army.

Spotting my wings and chute, he said, "Pardon me, but since you're a pilot, you wouldn't know how a fellow could hitch-hike a ride over to Foggia, would you? I missed the scheduled flight over there and find I can't leave now until tomorrow. My orders call for me to report today," said the major.

Looking over this major, I'm a bit speechless as I notice a large array of combat awards pinned on his tunic. The Distinguished Service Medal, Silver Star, Bronze Star with cluster, Purple Heart with two clusters. There were more, but I did not want to appear rude by staring. The major was just about the same age as I and he must have been through hell as an infantryman. "Well, Major, we are just a ferry outfit and not able to haul anyone since we only go one way and generally fly a single-seat ship," I said.

I could see the disappointment cross his face. "This is the first leave I have had for over two years," he said, "and it looks like I'm going to blow it all just trying to get to the rest camp area."

Warming up to the major, I started asking him questions about fighting as an infantryman at the front. I told him that I too had spent a year in combat as a fighter pilot and understood the problems. "Oh, by the way, Major, have you ever flown before?" I asked.

"Why no," he said, "I really admire you fly boys, it takes more guts than I got to go up there to dog-fight and get your ass shot at by both enemy ships and ground fire."

"I don't think that it's quite that bad, in fact I think that what you're doing is a lot worse," I replied. I then said to the major, "I am flying over to Foggia in about a half hour, I don't have a lot of room, but you are more than welcome to fly with me."

"Great," he said, "you just made my day. What kind of an airplane are we going in?" I pointed to the P-38 "Pathfinder" and said, "That one." His eyes got as big as saucers as he looked over at the '38.

Finishing up my flight plan and paperwork, I told him, "We should be leaving in about 20 minutes."

"Will I have time to go to the latrine?" he asks.

"You sure do," I said. I could see where the major was very nervous and as he talked to me his voice quivered a bit.

Returning from his little trip and less than five minutes later he said, "Do we still have a little time before we leave? I need to go to the bathroom again." This maneuver was repeated at least three more times. I can see him shaking and I feel sorry for him. Probably the best thing I can do is to get going, and he will soon be over this nervousness.

"Well, it's about that time," I tell him as he returns from his fourth trip. "Say, Major, what kind of flight would you like to have?" I ask.

"Would it be out of line if I asked you to fly like you would if you were on a combat mission? All the many hours of watching you guys," he says, "I have always wanted to see what it was actually like to really be there and do it."

"Fine," I say, "but it won't be real combat, just simulated," thinking I just wonder if he knows what he has let himself in for?

As I helped him enter the nose compartment, I showed him all the dials, radios, etc., and cautioned him not to screw around with anything, "Don't worry about a thing, I'll be in constant radio contact with you through this headseat," as I fastened it securely on his head. "I'll show you how it feels to be a fighter pilot on an armed recon run." He nods his head and waves good-by to me as I latch up the compartment door.

Hopping in the pilot's seat, I check out our intercom.

"Everything OK, Major?"

"Fine," comes the reply, "I'm ready."

In no time flat we are airborne and I point out all of the sights to him. Naples Bay, Vesuvius, mountains, etc., "By the way, Major, the flight will be less than 35 minutes."

"That's incredible," he says, "it would take me over a day to drive it." After clearing the area, I called the major and say, "Now the fun begins. We will go down to the deck like we usually do to avoid enemy radar and detection." As I push the nose down, I can imagine the major must be having quite a time in his front row seat.

I yelled into the inter-com in jest, "Major, at this low altitude we have no choice but to go under these approaching power lines."

"Oh my God!" gasped the major.

"Well, why not," I say and dive even lower to clear the lines. Zig-zagging over the countryside, I give the major a grand Cook's tour.

Coming up over one of the mountain peaks, I noticed down in the valley a B-17 on its belly. "I'll circle the Fort and see if they are all right," I tell him. Now in a very tight turn, we are really pulling some good "g's". I can see the crew waving and giving me the thumbs up signal. "You know something, Savage?" I say aloud. "Don't you think it's a bit strange that you haven't heard a peep out of your passenger?"

"Are you OK?" I call. No answer. Again I repeat only this time with a bit of concern, "*Major, are you OK?*" Still no answer. Oh well, maybe he is too busy enjoying everything.

Then I say, "Major, no flight would be complete without a victory roll," as I wind up our flight with a final victory roll.

Landing at the Foggia airport, I shut down and go forward to help my hitch-hiker friend deplane. Knocking on the small door, I call out, Major are you OK?" No answer.

My God! did I kill him?" I'm concerned now as I open up the compartment door. There sitting on his chair, wide-eyed, mouth ajar, speechless, is the Major.

Regaining his composure and speech, I expect to get my ass chewed out for putting on such a show. He says, "God, what a flight, my men at the front will never believe what I have just gone through."

"Sure they will," I said, as I ripped out a page from the Form 5 of the P-38 log book, with its data on the sheet.

Carefully, I asked this Major to spell his name to make sure I had everything right. I then wrote his name, rank and serial number, aircraft number, location, date and the trip description and stated: "On this day I,

Mark A. Savage ex-fighter pilot, 522 Squadron, of the 27th Fighter Bomber Group, did pick up this hitch-hiker and fly him in this P-38 "Pathfinder" from Naples, Italy, to Foggia, Italy, with a total flight time of 30 minutes." Then I signed my name, rank and serial number.

"I'll never forget this," he says, "but believe me, I'll take the infantry over the Air Corps any time," as he bids me farewell. . . .

"To each his own," I say solemnly in return.

Flight of P-38's patrolling the skies.
(Photo courtesy U.S. Air Force.)

Military version of the C-47 (DC-3)
(Photo courtesy U.S. Air Force Museum.)

Chapter 22
Do or Die

I had left Naples two days ago for a flight with one of the MATS C-47 airplanes from Naples to Athens, Green, then on to Cairo, Egypt, with an RON in Cairo.

We were to drop off some of our freight at the Athens airport and the remainder at Cairo. The Cairo flights were almost always made at night because of the heat generated this time of the year in Egypt. Earlier operations proved that if we landed anytime after 9:30 AM it would be almost physically impossible to even think about unloading the ship. The sun was so hot that if human flesh touched any metal parts the result produced a very painful burn.

Leaving Athens late that afternoon helped put us in Cairo during the cooler evening hours. I had made this run several times in the past and found it took two cigars and almost a half pack of cigarettes to complete this trip.

"Yea boy . . . this is the life," I said to my partner, Root. We'll split the legs on each flight, OK?"

"Roger," came back his reply. Weather presented no problem and it was smooth flying over the Adriatic & Mediterranean Seas on our way to Cairo. Visibility was excellent tonight and we spotted Cairo twenty plus miles out.

After landing and clearing the paper work, we checked into our BOQ and were glad to hit the sack.

Next morning we planned a tour of the Nile River, the Sphinx, and the Pyramids. Our Flight plan called for a day layover with an early morning departure the following day.

I had heard about the seven wonders of the world and was looking forward to visiting one of them. Being a tourist, I had to take the camel ride. *Never again!* They say it is like riding on a boat, *and it is!* My passenger seat rolled back-n-forth, left-n-right and I thought, Gosh, a guy could get mighty sea-sick with this rock-n-roll motion.

Standing in front and next to a pyramid makes a guy wonder just how did that huge thing get built way out here in the desert and by whom?

It was noon and the heat by now was so intense that both Root and I decided enough is enough as we retreated to the Officers Club and its cool bar.

Since I flew the last leg, Root took his turn as the Captain on the Cario to Naples run. I plotted the charts for our course, then filed the flight plan, after checking the weather. The metro officer advised that there was a weather system between us and our destination. He wasn't sure how severe, but he did know it would be instruments for several hours of this trip.

Checking over the aircraft manifest, I was amazed to find we had no cargo. All that was shown were two VIP's. A term used for (Very Important People).

A Colonel Zane, and a Wing Commander McArthur who were scheduled to fly from Cairo to Naples, Italy. "They must be pretty important to get their own ship," I remarked to Root as we got ready to depart.

Our clearance was simple. "You are cleared to Naples via your flight plan route." I had an ETA (expected time of arrival) of 4:55. Winds were on the nose and I was hoping we could do it in that projected time.

Flying from Egypt over Crete was quite uneventful. From Crete on we could see the start of the predicted clouds and weather off to the Northwest the same direction we were headed. Within an hour we caught the storm and entered it at 8,000 feet. Light rain at first, then heavy, much heavier than felt comfortable.

About twenty minutes later weather conditions started getting much worse as occasional lightning was observed. The air was becoming increasingly turbulent. Now from occasional bumps came very sharp jolts. "I don't like the way this storm is growing," I tell Root.

"Me either, I think we should be breaking out within a mile or two," he replied. Ten minutes later we are in the thick of it. We had no radar for help and we didn't know about or have airborne radar at that time. Out of range of all radio stations, we were on our own.

As we hit another string of down-drafts, Bob added power to try and maintain altitude. The ship is being tossed up, up to over 10,000 ft.

"Power full off!" Bob yells. "Drop the gear! Drop the gear!"

We're still going up and both Bob and I are on the controls fighting to keep the ship in some sort of controlled flight.

"This ship has turned into a beast," I yelled to Bob over the loud noise from the hard rain. He has no time to answer as we start another wild gyration. Up-Down, Up-Down, I have lost count. It seems like it is the end for sure.

The strong up-drafts end quickly but now we start down. "Pull up the gear, quick," yells Bob. *"Full power, full power."*

"I am! I am!" I yell as loud as I can, trying to make myself heard over all the pounding hail and rain.

Hard rain and hail are beating a tattoo on our metal body. We are both fighting for our very lives and the life of our ship. The windshield cracks on my side and water cascades in all over me, it looks grim.

"How much more do you think we can take?" I ask Root, who by now has his mouth and jaw clenched in a grim desperate position. Before he has a chance to answer we begin to repeat the same maneuvers. Up, down, power on, power off, gear up, gear down. Bob yells back to the radio man a Sergeant.

"Get on that radio and see if you can get a fix, and try to find out about this storm."

The Sergeant can hardly stay in his seat, and yells to Bob, *"I tried, sir, but there is too much static!"*

Our position is grim. "How much more can we take, Bob?" I yell. "According to my calculations we should be making the west coast of Italy just about right now, remember we have pretty high mountains immediately ahead."

Still in the fog and rain, he says, "You're right, let's turn now!"

Just about the time we completed our 180 degree turn, we break out into a completely clear area. Land is less than three miles away. The mountain tops are obscured by the heavy clouds, rain and fog. Circling in this small hole we have to make a decision.

"I don't think we have much choice, Bob, we will have to go back through it all again," I moan.

"You're right again, Doc," he says, "Let's do it, but before we go back in, let's see if we can get a message off to the base."

"Roger, that's a good idea," I said. The radio man lets out about 400 feet of antenna with its lead ball on the end in an effort to get word out about our position and predicament. He makes several calls and still no contact. Finally a faint message acknowledging our transmission and word that the weather is much better in Sicily is received. Encouraged by this we turn back into the storm determined to try and make Sicily.

Once again the same pounding fears and frustrations until we finally break out south of the storm.

Now somewhat in the clear, we try to estimate the visible damage. My front window has a large crack and both of us are soaking wet from all the leaks. I can hardly believe this ship has so many water leaks. Limping towards Sicily we call for landing info.

We went into that weather with an olive drab painted ship, now every visible leading edge is bent and dented. It's incredible! Further checking we are astounded: *We came out of this storm with our leading edges a shiny aluminum finish!* Catania Tower at Sicily gives us permission to land and we taxi up to the parking area. The mechanics report that it is a class 26 airplane. (Junk!) The main spar had a crack, and was bent, among a host of other things.

Since Bob and I got out of this alive, we both thank our God for sparing us. We received a special letter of commendation for our heroic action above and beyond the call of duty that said in part, "You are to be congratulated for the skillful handling of the airplane . . . etc., etc."

Yes, skill did play a part, a small part. The most important factor in that flight was either, *"Do or Die!"*

NAPOLI – PANORAMA DELLA CITTA VISTO DALLA VILLA PATRIZI

Vesuvius erupting, Naples, Italy, 1944.

Chapter 23
"I'm With Who?"

Vesuivius is the name of that huge volcano located south-east of Naples. It sure looked like it might become active just about any time. The last time it blew its top was the year of '79 AD when it erupted without notice and in turn completely destroyed and buried the city of Pompeii.

We, MATS (Military Air Transport Service-328 Ferry Squadron) had one of our major bases located at the Capodochino Airport in Naples, right next to Vesuivius. It was one of the main staging areas for supplying the war machine in the southern part of Europe.

Our group had been flying up to Naples on an average of about three times a week. Nearby on the southeast base of Vesuivius was a B-25 medium bomber group. There was always a lot of activity in this area with the ships going to and from the battle zones.

For the past couple of months we had been ferrying P-38's up to Naples from Casablanca. This just happened to be my third trip with a P-38 in the past two weeks.

We all worked as a team and we tried to constantly watch for conditions that might affect our safety. We still had a bunch of P-38's to get to Naples and it was getting more difficult every day due to Vesuivius's increased activity. Vesuivius was smoking day and night and was acting like it was about ready to blow its top.

The whole valley was slowly filling up with smoke and making flying very tough. Occasionally when the wind came off the bay of Naples, we were able to get fair visibilities and flying conditions. It appeared that the threat was over now and it was the early part of the week when it finally happened.

Vesuivius blew its top!

Despite all those signs, rumblings, constant ashes and smoke, the warning was not heeded. The Commander of the B-25 Group with three Squadrons based at the airport next to the volcano failed to order an evacuation of his group. Vesuivius now in its full fury was spewing out hot lava directly towards the base.

The B-25 Group officers were often at the club bar with us. They constantly assured us that their base was in no danger. "But aren't you guys just a little bit concerned?" I asked.

"No way, remember the town that was destroyed called Pompeii? Well, it just won't happen to us, since we are on the other side of the volcano," said one of the Squadron pilots.

Now Vesuivius in its full fury spewed molten lava and out of its ruptured side. The molten material heads directly for the airstrip. "How can they be so stupid?" asks Crabtree.

"Beats me," I said as we watch mother nature flex her muscles.

Word has yet to be given to the Group as now it looks like it's only a matter of hours before the molten lava will be at their front door. While we were at the Orange Club, the Officers Club located high on a hill overlooking the volcano, we felt a big rumble and then saw one huge fire ball leap out from the top of the volcano. Hot cinders and ash followed as Vesuivius got quite violent.

A frantic call to the club requesting all personnel of the B-25 Group to immediately report back to base. The B-25's must be moved now or face destruction. It was too late, the lava broke through and started covering the runway. Within an hour the lava rapidly started eating up the parked B-25's. Incredible, how could this happen? Well it did, and now several ships are almost completely covered by the hot molten lava. "Someone is going to catch hell on this one," said Prouty.

"You can say that again," I replied.

The next day we were back on the shuttle to Casablanca, but our thoughts were still on the active Vesuivius. Every minute there was truly spectacular, but orders are orders and we had to leave. Arriving in Casablanca, we could see another batch of new P-38's ready and waiting for us to deliver.

The usual procedure was followed and I was on my way the next day bound for Naples. "It's going to be a bit rough going to Naples now," I said to Jack Dollard while checking weather and preparing the flight plan.

"How's that?" said Jack. "Oh that dumb volcano blew its top the other day and has put the visibility down to less than a mile, and it could give us fits when we try to find Naples and the airport," I replied.

"Well all we can do is wait and see," he said, unconcerned.

Flying the P-38 at 12,000 feet and in the clear towards Naples, I could easily see the smoke from the active volcano. I first spotted the smoke as far away as Sicily.

As I got closer to Naples, I called the Capodichino Tower.

"Capo Tower, this is Air Force P-38 November 347 calling and requesting the local conditions and landing information. By the way, how bad has the volcano been acting up today?" I said.

"Pretty bad," they replied, "and the visibility here is down to less than a mile. We have your request for landing and now request you change your radio frequency to GCA."

"Roger," I replied switching over and wondering silently just what the hell he meant, and what is G.C.A.?

Calling this new frequency, my radio snapped back a reply with this really clipped true English type voice. "Hello old chap, Air Force November 347, a P-38, right? Do you read me?"

"Roger, loud and clear," I reply.

"Good, you're with GCA here," comes the reply.

"I understand, I think, but what is GCA?" I ask.

"You have nothing to worry about, you are in our hands now with our brand new GCA (Ground Control Approach). In fact we can help you down through this muck to a safe approach, but it will be up to you to land your ship."

"Of course, this system is quite new and we want you to be aware of it," he adds.

Sitting on top of this solid undercast now at 12,000 feet in the blue sky, I am faced with a decision. I ask myself, "Do I trust this guy and go through with this, or go back to North Africa?" Well, I have decided. "No, I don't know anything at all about this GCA business, so therefore I would feel much better not doing it, and I will go back."

Almost reading my mind, the radio now barks out an order, "Air Force November 347, turn left to a heading of 030 degrees, and advise when you are steady on this new heading. Please confirm your present altitude."

An order is an order and I turn to obey, still not convinced I want to go through with this. "Relax, we now have you identified as a positive target and you will be told what to do," he says.

"How the hell can they do that?" I tell myself, quite unsure of just what to expect next.

"OK, November 347, turn left now to a gyro heading of 300 degrees."

"Roger," I said and complied with his request.

I'm still up here in the crystal blue sky with all that murk and gloom down below me. Not a comfortable feeling to think I am putting my life on a system unknown and unproven as far as I am concerned.

"November 347, this is GCA here, we will be starting you down in about 10 miles."

"Roger," I reply and wonder, are they that sure they know where I am? If they make a mistake, I'll end up smashing into the mountains of Italy.

"OK, November 347, you are to start your let-down now at a standard rate of 500 feet per minute." I don't exactly feel comfortable putting my life on a system unknown and unproven as far as I am concerned.

I'm immediately snapped out of my thoughts by the voice that says, "We show you are now well out over the water and you can safely let down and be able to make ground contact."

Really now, I think, *can they be absolutely sure?*

Another call, this time just a bit irritated, "November 347, we show you thirty miles west of Naples out over the Med. Have you started down yet?"

"No . . . not yet," I reply.

"We suggest that you start down, NOW!"

"Well it's now or never," I think. "Those guys down there just don't give up."

Putting approach flaps down, with reduced speed, I am now able to drop my gear, and I start down into the soup. 8, 6, 5 thousand feet, it seems like hours since I last saw the blue sky and sun. Even if I am lucky, I know I won't see anything until I am at least 1,000 feet above, I hope, the water.

Four-three-two-one thousand feet, still nothing. I'll hold at 1,000 feet and maybe I'll break out. "*Altimeter!! . . . did I get an altimeter setting?*" A fine time to have doubts now. "Yes, I remember, I did get one just before they started telling me to begin my let down."

The unknown voice calls me again, "Have you broken out yet, and what is your altitude and flight conditions?"

Before I have a chance to answer, I'm down now to 800 feet and just barely able to see a few white caps on the water. God, what a good feeling!

Calling GCA, I advised them, "I have made visual contact." Well, at least I'm alive and inbound with some semblance of ground references as I peer through the dense smoke now covering the whole area.

"Roger," they reply, "now turn east to a 095 degree heading and this should take you to the airport that we show to be about forty miles from you. You may now call Capo Tower for further clearance to land. *Oh, by the way old chap! before we sign off, we appreciate your taking the time to practice with us.*"

Practice? . . . Practice? . . . with GCA! . . . what practice?

Believe me, *this was for real.*

Airplane depot located at Pomigliano, Italy 1944. P-38's, P-47's, P-51's, and A-26's.
According to US Army Weather Service, "History of Air Weather Service, 1943-45" (typescript, 1945) AMS Bulletin 60, no 2 (1979) 182-83. In mid-March 1944, eighty-six bombers valued at approximately $25-30 million dollars were destroyed when Vesuvius erupted.

**Sentimental Journey in the Curtiss "Commando" C-46
(Photo courtesy U.S. Air Force Museum.)**

Chapter 24
Sentimental Journey

War in Europe had come to an end. V.E. (Victory in Europe). The war had also ended in Asia. V.J. (Victory over Japan). Having enough points, I could elect to go home almost any time of my choosing. I was enjoying flying all over Europe and in no particular rush to go home. In fact, there was a great proposition facing me to volunteer for an extended tour as Operations Officer in Weisbaden, Germany. "Why not?" I thought. Another year or so here now is not that bad and it would mean a promotion to Major within a year.

The younger officers of the Squadron thought I had been here too long and flipped, since I did not want to go home to the USA. Every evening at the officer's club bar the kids would say, "Hey Doc, you have enough points, why don't you hang it up and go on home?"

"Chad" Chadbourne and I were close friends and we agonized many long hours on whether we should or should not leave for the States. Both he and I were dating pretty nurses at the 300th General Hospital, what more could a guy want?

Within a week our idealistic lifestyle changed. Both gals informed us they had orders to ship out and back to the States. Their departing words were, "See you all State-side soon." Chad was quite serious about nurse Hilda and began selling me on, "You know, Doc, we have been over here for quite some time, almost three years, maybe we have forgotten what the U.S. is like."

After about three weeks of pressure by Chad and the younger kids, I finally said, "Oh, what the hell, maybe you guys are right after all."

There had been a massive program launched that was aimed at air-lifting as many troops back home as possible. The 328th had shifted to the Curtiss C-46 "Commando" and after flying the Douglas C-47 (DC-3) for over a year, I was not too keen nor happy flying the C-46. Sure it hauled a real heavy load, but, boy, did we have the mechanical problems with it. Very few of us were comfortable or felt completely relaxed while flying the 46. It had so many mechanical problems that it was a nightmare most of the time.

Each new group was assigned a ship, usually the C-47, and they immediately prepared to leave for the good old USA. I began to feel that I had better get on the list to go home.

After all, flying the C-47 was a piece of cake and I was anxious to get back to it again. Both Chad and I put in for a transfer and to no surprise found our names together at the top of the list to leave.

With our new orders cut, we were assigned, (surprise) a C-46 to fly home. "What a cruel blow," I told Chad as we prepared our ship for the long trip home.

"Well, you're right, Doc, but it's better than going back by boat." My mind flashed back to the 25 days spent on the Colin P. Kelly Liberty ship trip, and I had no other excuse but to accept this assignment.

Signing the papers for our ship, we soon found that we were assigned 40 infantrymen as passengers. They were all from the 5th Army and none below the rank of Sergeant.

Loading up, we were all in a good mood since we knew our final destination would be the USA. Looking over the list of passengers, I was a youngster compared to these infantrymen. Most of them had at least five years overseas; you could count the hash marks on their sleeves. They all had lots of ribbons and awards of all kinds. Several had been through the entire war from North Africa, Italy, France and Germany. They were tough and didn't give a damn and they showed it.

I briefed them on this trip by saying, "It's going to be a long trip with many long boring hours of overwater flying. We will do our best to keep you all advised and, by the way, you all are more than welcome to come up on the flight deck and ask questions. That is, a couple of men at a time."

"Sure, sure," was the half-hearted response. Leaving Naples for the last time, we swung out towards our first stop, Casablanca. Half way there, we started developing a serious problem. The ship was getting harder and harder to fly because the auto pilot just went out. "Great," I said to Chad, "I hope that this is not an omen."

"No way," says Chad, and just about this time the hydraulic boost pump lets go. Now we have no aileron boost and the airplane really starts flying like a heavy overloaded truck half out of control. "I don't think it is real serious," says Chad, it appears to be the usual hydraulic leak.

"Perhaps we can get some work done at Casablanca," I said. We both had to fly it as it took a lot of strength to keep it on a straight course.

We blew several days in Casablanca as the mechanics worked on our ship. Word finally came that they found the problem so we can take off tomorrow.

Rounding up our passengers proved to be quite a task since they were out to see as much of the city as they could. We even feared for their lives and told them as much prior to their leaving. We made sure they knew about the problems of going alone into the Casbah. It wasn't the romantic scenes that Bogart and Bacall made it out to be in the movie, "Casablanca," including the very beautiful song he sang (?) called, "As time goes by."

Loaded up, we departed Casa for Dakar, our next stop. On landing at this remote field, we were met by the tallest blacks I have ever seen. With their bright red fez's everyone of them appeared to be close to 7 feet tall. They were very friendly and we were able to communicate through the use of pidgin English.

Our next leg stop was Roberts, South Africa. Prior to landing we heard a terrible commotion in the back of the ship. I went aft to the passenger section and found better than three-quarters of the men stoned on the booze they had picked up at our last stop. No good talking to them now, so I went up front and advise Chad about the situation.

On landing, we confiscated all the bottles and threw them out, with a stern warning. "Men, starting tomorrow we're about to embark on the most dangerous part of our trip. Seven hours out over the Atlantic Ocean to the Ascension Islands. We just can't have you in this condition."

"But Sir, if we do go down, we won't have much of a chance as a snow ball in hell of being rescued, right, Sir?" I couldn't openly agree with him but right he is.

"It doesn't make much sense. How can you even hope to survive if you're all dead drunk?" I said. I know I did not sound too convincing even to myself, but I had to say it.

"Yes, Sir, but at least we all will be happy." A roar of laughter greets that remark.

Starting out over the water the next day, we have no doubt about our making Ascension. Now six hours later, tension mounts knowing that we only have 45 minutes reserve if we miss that little four by five piece of rock located out in the middle of the Atlantic. Both Chad and I had our navigator shoot a celestial plot at least three times to reassure us that we were on course. We were doubly concerned since our navigator hadn't done any real celestial navigation in over two years. A mistake out here could be fatal.

Desperately tuning in our low freq radio, we faintly hear a signal. Soon the ADF needle begins to quiver and point. Now the signal gets stronger and positively identified, we find that airport on the island in the ocean.

From Ascension on to Brazil, South America. Tuning in our short wave radio, we start picking up a broadcast from the U.S. mainland.

One song in particular is being played at this time. We plug into the cabin speakers for all the men to hear . . . *Sentimental Journey.* "What beautiful timing! I'll never forget that," I say to Chad. "Me either," quips Chad.

Another stop now and we are in the steaming jungles of Belem on the Amazon River. Wild animals cry and roar all night. "Boy, I'll be glad to get out of here," says Chad.

Flying from Belem up to Puerto Rico puts us over a green jungle area that stretches for miles and miles. Occasionally we see a native grass hut in a small clearing. Once in a while about a dozen or so huts appear that make up a village.

"God, I sure would hate to go down anywhere around here: we would never get out alive," I mention to Chad. He tried to soft pedal this, but I knew he was just as concerned as I.

A few more hours of instrument flying in the heavy rains with an occasional thunderstorm thrown in, when finally, we pop out in the clear and away from this equatorial front. A wet front that girdles the center part of the earth, better known as the equator. This front generally produces copious amounts of rain almost daily in this Amazon rain forest.

Flying on up past Trinidad, then Cuba and finally, ten days later, we are ready to touch down at Morrison Field, West Palm Beach, Florida. "What a sight! It's good to be back to the USA in one piece," Chad says, as we lined up for our approach to landing. We received our clearance and made ready to land. The crew chief is anxious and asks permission to drop the gear. Well why not? It's been a long time and we are quite willing to share with everyone the enthusiasm of being home in the USA.

On the final approach and less than a quarter mile from the field, the tower advises, *"Go around, go around, there is a small plane that just popped up in front of you."*

"Roger," we reply and comply with the command. Before we can say or do a thing, the crew chief pulls up the gear and flaps at the same time. We're using full power but sinking fast, it looks like we will be hitting the ground for sure. At the very last moment, the props take hold and we skim the ground by inches. Still shaking we swing around for that last final landing. We both decided not to chew this guy out. After all, this is our first time home for most of us in many years.

Checking in at the motel, Chad says, "Say Doc, I have a spot on the Beach where we can get a frozen daquiri and ogle the pretty girls."

"Why not," I say, "but what the hell is a frozen daquiri?"

"You haven't lived until you try it," he says as we make our way to the beach.

Could be I was hungry, hot or both, but those daquiries hit the spot. In the air conditioned bar, we found those pretty girls to ogle. After about the fifth daquiri I said to Chad, "I think it's about time to go eat."

"Right on, Doc, I know just the place." He leads the way out of this air conditioned bar and up the hot sandy beach to a real nice restaurant located down the beach.

I hadn't taken ten steps when I just about collapsed. Chad came to my rescue and helped me back to the motel. I wasn't fit to eat, or ogle anything at this time. But I rebounded in a few hours and thanked God for the opportunity to make that, *Sentimental Journey*.